teach®

yourself

ship

and

pson

than

over

urself

be where you want to be
with **teach yourself**

For UK order enquiries: please contact Bookpoint Ltd, 130 Milton Park, Abingdon, Oxon, OX14 4SB. Telephone: +44 (0) 1235 827720. Fax: +44 (0) 1235 400454. Lines are open 09.00–17.00, Monday to Saturday, with a 24-hour message answering service. Details about our titles and how to order are available at www.teachyourself.co.uk

For USA order enquiries: please contact McGraw-Hill Customer Services, PO Box 545, Blacklick, OH 43004-0545, USA. Telephone: 1-800-722-4726. Fax: 1-614-755-5645.

For Canada order enquiries: please contact McGraw-Hill Ryerson Ltd, 300 Water St, Whitby, Ontario, L1N 9B6, Canada. Telephone: 905 430 5000. Fax: 905 430 5020.

Long renowned as the authoritative source for self-guided learning – with more than 50 million copies sold worldwide – the **teach yourself** series includes over 500 titles in the fields of languages, crafts, hobbies, business, computing and education.

British Library Cataloguing in Publication Data: a catalogue record for this title is available from the British Library.

Library of Congress Catalog Card Number: on file.

First published in UK 2007 by Hodder Education, part of Hachette Livre UK, 338 Euston Road, London, NW1 3BH.

First published in US 2007 by The McGraw-Hill Companies, Inc.

This edition published 2007.

The **teach yourself** name is a registered trade mark of Hodder Headline.

Typeset by Transet Limited, Coventry, England.
Printed in Great Britain for Hodder Education, part of Hachette Livre UK, 338 Euston Road, London, NW1 3BH, by Cox & Wyman Ltd, Reading, Berkshire.

The publisher has used its best endeavours to ensure that the URLs for external websites referred to in this book are correct and active at the time of going to press. However, the publisher and the author have no responsibility for the websites and can make no guarantee that a site will remain live or that the content will remain relevant, decent or appropriate.

Hachette Livre UK's policy is to use papers that are natural, renewable and recyclable products and made from wood grown in sustainable forests. The logging and manufacturing processes are expected to conform to the environmental regulations of the country of origin.

Impression number   10 9 8 7 6 5 4 3 2
Year   2012 2011 2010 2009 2008

contents

Note

The authors would be happy to respond to queries and you can contact them via: catherine.doherty@fieldsoflearning.com

01

everybody can be, and everybody is, a leader

In this chapter we will consider how to:
- acknowledge your potential to grow to be the leader you desire to be
- explore how you want to be viewed as a leader
- listen to what others said about a noted leader

Introduction

> '*Personally, I'm always ready to learn although I do not always like being taught.*'
>
> Winston Churchill

Wouldn't it be fantastic to be able to learn in a way that suits you and be able to apply that learning immediately, to practical benefit and to understand why what you then do enables you to lead with effectiveness and impact?

> '*Leadership is something that can be learned by anyone, taught to everyone, denied to no-one.*'
>
> Bennis and Nanus from
> *Leaders: Strategies for Taking Charge*

A manager asked his mentor 'What do I have to do to be a better leader?' The mentor replied: 'It is not the *doing*, it is the *being* that counts.' So how does one **be** a better leader? Everyone has within them the ability to be the best leader they can be. This book aims to unlock some of the most successful techniques used by leaders to help you go beyond even what you dreamt you could be.

The attributes of leaders are not in a formula. We do not have a little list of things to do to be a great leader. What we do have is a series of techniques that will unlock in you the qualities that you already have to lead, and which will introduce you to the experience of other key leadership behaviours that you can develop.

Leadership is not a thing. You cannot pick it up, fill a wheelbarrow with it, or buy it. Leadership is the ability to lead; the ability to generate ideas, communicate them and create the belief in followers that the idea or mission is worthwhile.

Leaders are all around us. Some leaders have a title – Prime Minister, President, Chief Executive, Headmistress, Conductor, Captain. Some demonstrate leadership over a long period of time – matriarch, founder of the family business, political idealist, general, head of nursing.

Some show leadership in the moment and we sometimes call them heroes, as they seem to take charge of impossible situations and lead people through them – the nursery teacher who led her children to safety in the face of a knife attack, or the passenger in a capsizing ferry who convinced others to join him to create a human bridge over which many could scramble to a place of rescue.

Leadership is not a function of age. There is not an age at which you become old enough to lead. Children can lead and do it with unconscious ease. They have ideas, they tell their friends about the idea and their friends want to do it, and will undertake extraordinary feats to be part of the leading child's adventure.

The qualities that make followers want to support the leader are not the same in every circumstance. There is no secret list to be shared. The secrets to our potential are inside us. This book will tell you how to unlock your own ability to lead.

Just because someone is a leader it doesn't mean they are a nice person

We can think of leaders who may have created following but we perceived their mission or outcome was flawed: Saddam Hussein, Sven Goran Erikson (the ex-England Football Manager), and President Mugabe of Zimbabwe. This book gives us ways of cross-referencing our own missions, identities, beliefs and values, which in turn influence the skills and capabilities and individual behaviour as well as the environments in which we choose to lead. This book gives leaders valuable ways of eliciting feedback from others to ensure they harvest the perspectives of critical friends and not just the adoration of submissive or intimidated followers. Many flawed leaders on the world stage did not have critical feedback, and were viewed by followers as demi-gods. Hitler had no one to provide feedback, whereas many who succeeded did – Shackleton had Wild, Nixon had Kissinger, and Queen Victoria had Prince Albert.

How are you leading now?

It may be that you are not leading in the way that you want to lead. You may not be achieving the outcomes that are important to you. Then again, you may disagree and feel that your leadership meets the needs of the moment.

If you keep leading in the way that you currently do you will keep arriving at the place that you currently arrive. This may or may not be where you want to be.

> 'None of us knows what the next change is going to be, what unexpected opportunities are just around the corner, waiting a few months or a few years to change all the tenor of our lives.'
>
> Kathleen Norris

This book unlocks secrets of motivation, flexibility and creating choices that make for excellence in leadership and that allow us to continue to achieve results in different circumstances. We do this by tuning the skills and awareness inside ourselves rather than practising leadership according to a set of pre-determined tasks. Leadership is about being, not about doing.

As you read on you will be helped to unlock the genius, power and magic in yourself and will be taken beyond your current expectations of what you can achieve as a leader.

The book explores leading with the help of some *voices* of leaders who have been remarkable and voices of people who are just like us. You will learn techniques, hear stories and recognize styles of leadership that can give insight, confidence and new skills to enable you as a leader to be your best, to lead in a way that is right for you and for those you seek to lead.

Your path to success as a leader is laid out in this book. You can be your best. Each step will enable you to:

- know what 'the right' leadership is like for you
- focus on what you really want to achieve
- focus on knowing yourself better than you ever have and know that you can prepare to lead in the way you want to
- influence and relate with others
- create the balance you need in your life to lead and remain the person you want to be

The voice of Nelson Mandela at his inauguration speech as President in 1994 gives a moment of great inspiration by quoting the words of Marianne Williamson.

'Our deepest fear is not that we are inadequate. Our deepest fear is that we are powerful beyond measure.

It is our light, not our darkness that frightens us.

We ask ourselves, "Who am I to be brilliant, gorgeous, talented and fabulous?" Actually, who are you not to be? You are a child of God. Your playing small doesn't serve the world.

There is nothing enlightened about shrinking so that other people won't feel insecure around you.

We were born to make manifest the glory of God that is within us. It is not just in some of us, it is in everyone.

And as we let our own light shine, we unconsciously give other people permission to do the same.

*As we are liberated from our fear, our presence
automatically liberates others.'*

Let the journey begin

Your first step to be the leader you want to be, is to come on a
journey into the future. When you see how much you can
achieve you can begin to head for that place. If you don't know
where you are going you may end up somewhere else. In *Alice in
Wonderland*, the cat makes this point to Alice. Alice asks,
'Would you tell me please, which way I am to go from here?'
'That depends a great deal on where you want to get to,' said the
cat. 'I don't much care where ...' said Alice. 'Then it doesn't
matter which way you go,' said the cat.

So where do you want to be as a leader? You can look into the
future and make these choices. Imagine you are Ann, a leader
who is saying goodbye to her team of the last ten years. You are
a fly on the wall and you can hear all that people are saying
about Ann. You look down and you see all the people at the
event. You notice how they are interacting with each other and
you hear what they are saying about the woman as a leader ...

'She was great but she never really achieved what she was
capable of ...'

'She did a great job and yet there was something more that I
believed she could have done ...'

'I have no idea if she believed in me and my abilities ...'

'She once talked about her dream and then she got so busy doing
things that I never really found out what that dream was ...
Maybe she can achieve it in her next job.'

'I liked her and yet I never felt I knew her.'

Ann, who is at the point of completing her leadership of this
task, has not heard the words from others that she would like to
have heard used to describe her as a leader. Such an experience
of eavesdropping would inevitably leave her (or any of us)
disappointed. She would much rather have heard them saying
things like:

'She allowed me to connect with her ideas and then really play
my part in my way ...'

'She inspired me to believe that I was capable of more than I
realized and gave me the confidence to do that ...'

'Her inspirational ideas and belief in the outcome she wanted to achieve were so compelling we all got behind her ...'

'Change and new ideas never phased her ... she always had a clear picture of what we could achieve ...'

'She was great!'

Albert Einstein proposed, '*Imagination is more important than knowledge*'. We can use this ability to imagine or foresee a situation before we commit others and ourselves to it. Einstein went on to say '*When I examine myself and my methods of thought, I come to the conclusion that the gift of fantasy has meant more to me than my talent for absorbing positive knowledge.*'

You will already know of many leading sportsmen or women who use future thinking and visualization of what they want to achieve as a major part of their preparation. Sally Gunnell, an Olympic Hurdle Champion, has been heard to describe how she would visualize running her race hundreds of times a day in the months leading to her next race. This everyday technique of using your imagination to explore ideas, outcomes and scenarios is a powerful way to test them before you embark on them.

EXERCISE

Leave things as they are

Imagine now that you change nothing about your current leadership and that this is your finishing party, and you are the fly on the wall. You will know how far into the future represents the place where this event will take place. What will people be saying about you? You may also want to listen to your own voice projecting its judgement on you too. As you listen to all these voices now you may also be formalizing your excuses for not achieving your potential.

This part of the exercise can give you a 'wake up call' and help you to realize that what you are doing now may or may not be getting you the results that you want and if you had the opportunity in the future to re-run your past actions you could take some different steps.

Create the future you want to see

Now go to that same point in the future. This time you magically arrive there and the experience and achievements you have had in

---

between now and this future point have been fantastic. Everything has turned out well. What will people now be saying about you and the way you led them? What will they say about your sense of purpose, the vision you projected for them to see? The beliefs that you held, and the skilful and capable way that you led them? What sort of environment did you create for them to succeed? This scenario is your dream come true.

Like Sally Gunnell, imagine it in some detail to make it even more real. Notice what you see around you, who will be there, how they will be standing and milling about with others. Notice even how the venue, the food and the ambience are exactly what you would like.

Hear now the pitch of the conversations, the tone of voice people have as they discuss with others the difference that you made to them and the projects they worked on. Hear the words they use to describe you and the ring of truth that is in them as they really mean what they say about the positive things you did.

As you see and hear all this, experience how it feels to know that you have achieved what you wanted, what you really wanted and then even a little bit more. Enjoy the sense of pride and confidence telling you that you have done an exceptional job and that even you know it. Enjoy the moment, as it represents real achievement of your goal.

So as you harvest the comments you can hear being made from your fly-on-the-wall perspective, you can also begin to imagine the types of steps you will need to take to achieve this wonderful experience that you have just had of people valuing you as a leader.

What you have done in this exercise is to step into experiencing your achievement of your goals. From this you look back at and recognize the things that you need to do to ensure that you have the sort of success that you want. The sort that will have you feeling the best you can about yourself, knowing that you have met your own goals and criteria for success. You can make it happen right now.

Make a note of those steps now. As you work through this book, it would be useful to have a notebook handy to use for the exercises and to jot down points.

You will now know that there are things you want to develop about your leadership. *Teach Yourself Leadership* is like a critical and supportive friend helping you, giving you advice, tips and feedback that will make you the leader you want to be, the leader you are capable of being.

This book will show you how others have learned to become great leaders and will give you the techniques to break through the barriers that can hold you back. Once the barriers are removed you can learn the techniques that will propel you forward.

Throughout the book you will hear from other leaders using the idea of 'voices'. After each 'voice', you will join in an analysis of what has been said: you will see how the idea applies to one of the techniques for improving your learning and leadership, then have the opportunity to do an exercise to get a feel for things for yourself. In each chapter we will tell you what the chapter has in store for you, and at the end we summarize the key success points.

Now that you know what treasures the book holds for you, let us introduce you to Sir Ernest Shackleton, the Antarctic explorer, as an example of what great leaders do. We will explore his different styles of leadership in Chapter 2.

Margaret Morrell and Stephanie Capparell in their book *Shackleton's Way* describe Shackleton 'as the greatest leader on God's earth bar none' for saving the lives of 27 men stranded with him on an Antarctic ice floe for almost two years. Yet they pose the paradox that he failed to reach every goal he ever set. He failed to reach the South Pole in 1902 with Scott. In 1907 he turned back 97 miles from the Pole. On his expedition to cross the South Pole, in 1914, Shackleton and his men were wrecked when their ship was crushed by ice. Shackleton did not even technically reach Antarctica on this expedition. Yet his entire crew survived despite being stranded 1,200 miles from civilization and without communication. They survived on penguin, seals and finally their husky dogs. When the ice began to break up they dragged three rowing boats across the ice floes for five months. When the floes began to break up they sailed and rowed 60 miles and found Elephant Island and made camp. Shackleton then set out with five men and endured 17 days of storms as they got back to South Georgia only to be wrecked on the opposite side of the island to the civilization of the whaling station.

He was then faced with crossing the uncharted mountains to arrive at the station and when he arrived he had to plan how to charter a boat to return to Elephant Island to pick up his stranded men. After several failed attempts he made it and collected them all alive and well.

So, as we explore the lessons from Shackleton and other leaders, enjoy the discovery for you that this book holds, the discovery that lies within you. Just applying one quarter of the techniques and ideas within the book will stretch your mind, and your perceptions, and a mind once stretched never returns to its previous shape.

Learning for leadership success

- You have considered yourself as being a leader
- You know what others will value in you
- You have begun to imagine what you need to do to achieve your leadership outcomes
- You have heard of the impact that Sir Ernest Shackleton had on those who followed him

Reflections on a leader

From those who knew Shackleton.

'His method of discipline was very fair. He did not believe in unnecessary discipline.'

William Bakewell, seaman, *Endurance*

'I almost found him rising to his best and inspiring confidence when things were at their blackest.'

Frank Hurley, photographer, *Endurance*

'I do not think there is any doubt that we all owe our lives to his leadership and his power to make a loyal and coherent party out of rather diverse elements.'

Reginald W. James, physicist, *Endurance*

'No matter what turns up, he is always ready to alter his plans and make fresh ones, and in the meantime, jokes, and enjoys a joke with anyone, and in this way keeps everyone's spirits up.'

Frank Worsley, Captain, *Endurance*

'He was a tower of strength and endurance, and he never panicked in any emergency.'

Walter How, seaman and sail maker, *Endurance*

'He was essentially a fighter, afraid of nothing and of nobody, but, withal, he was human, overflowing with kindness and generosity, affectionate and loyal to all his friends.'

Louis C. Bernacchi, physicist, *Discovery*

'He led, he did not drive.'

G. Vibert Douglas, geologist, *Quest*

02

seven styles of leading

In this chapter you will:
- be clear that there is not one best leadership style
- understand your current leadership style
- be introduced to other leadership styles, and when they may be useful
- have explained how the techniques in following chapters support your leadership attempts

'Ultimately, Shackleton is a success because, in him, we catch glimpses of who we want to be.'
Jonathan Karpoff, University of Washington

Introduction

The answer to the question 'How do I become a leader?' is elusive. Professor Bernie Bass has identified over 3,000 studies on leadership. During the 1990s, 10 academic papers a day were being published on the topic. And the conclusion is that there is no one leadership style that fits all circumstances. Studies of 'great' leaders that explore their personality, characteristics and qualities do not give the answer either. Ralph Stodgill in the 1950s conducted a study of 'great' leaders to identify their common characteristics. His findings were inconclusive. He found 'that 50 years of study have failed to produce one personality trait or set of qualities that can discriminate between leaders and non-leaders'.

Any hunt for the answer to leadership is further confounded by an examination of the biography of leaders, who were often successful at some times and not at others, for example:

- Churchill is seen as a great war leader during the Second World War. Yet he was viewed as a failure in the 1930s, and was rejected by the British people, losing the General Election in 1945.
- Margaret Thatcher was seen as a great leader in her prime from 1979. She was unceremoniously dumped in 1991 by those who had been her followers.
- In sport, a soccer coach, Brian Clough, took two teams, Derby County and Nottingham Forest, to success at home and in European competition. He left to lead another club, Leeds United. That team memorably rejected him in 40 days. He then resumed a successful career at Nottingham.

Another factor that makes the hunt for the answer problematic is that in many ways and at many times each of you have been a leader, whether you have led a sports team to success, had success with a project, made a successful sales presentation, or created a well-working business team. The question is whether what you have done in the past will be appropriate for what you wish to achieve in the future.

Your current leadership style

Why do you need to explore your current understanding of your leadership style? Malcolm Knowles in his studies on adult learning has shown that adults must build on and shift their old patterns to absorb new understanding. You will know this is true when someone tells you how to do something you already know. Your reaction is likely to be 'why should I change – I already know this and I resent someone asking me to change my pattern!' So you may not change. You may not know that there are other ways. To change and learn you must explore your current view of leadership, compare your view to others' views, and where there is a gap that you wish to fill, you will take action to learn. Your first step is to explore your current understanding.

EXERCISE: Leadership Styles – Self

You will have read the quotations in Chapter 1 about the range of leadership styles that Shackleton's followers observed. This exercise allows you to identify your perception of the styles you use most, and use least. Listed below are some statements about leadership behaviour. Indicate how often you engage in the behaviours, using the scale below to respond to each statement. Please place a number from 0 to 4 in the space beside each question.

The numbers 0 to 4 have the following meaning:

0 = never
1 = hardly ever
2 = sometimes
3 = fairly often
4 = frequently, if not always

1 _____ I give a clear vision of what we need to accomplish.

2 _____ I provide followers with a clear view of the goals we want to achieve.

3 _____ I inspire others by focusing on the values and beliefs of the team.

4 _____ put forward ideas that challenge my follower's ideas to provide them with the stimulation to change.

5 _____ I intervene only when there is a problem.

6 _____ I give my followers a reward when they succeed.

7 _____ I coach each follower to succeed.

8 _____ I only change things when they go wrong.

9 _____ I act as the 'motivator' for my team.

10 _____ I make it clear to my followers what they have to do to be rewarded.

11 _____ I mentor each follower.

12 _____ I allow my followers to decide how to reach their goals.

13 _____ I am viewed as someone who others wish to follow.

14 _____ I help my followers to look at their problems differently to provide resourceful choices.

15 _____ provide my followers with the opportunity to do their best.

16 _____ I give rewards and promotions for excellent performance.

17 _____ I advise each follower.

18 _____ I make sure followers know when they have achieved their goals.

19 _____ I encourage rational problem solving.

20 _____ I believe I have gained the respect and trust of my followers.

21 _____ I make sure followers have evidence of goal achievement.

Scoring

Now transfer your responses above to the scoring sheet below, which has three questions for each of seven leadership styles, and total your results.

Management by Exception

Q.5 _____

Q.8 _____

Q.18 _____

Total _____

Contingent Reward

Q.6 _____

Q.10 _____

Q.16 _____

Total _____

Management through Objectives

Q.2 _____

Q.12 _____

Q.21 _____

Total _____

Intellectual Stimulation

Q.4 _____

Q.14 _____

Q.19 _____

Total _____

Inspirational

Q.3 _____

Q.9 _____

Q.15 _____

Total _____

Individualized Consideration

Q. 7 _____

Q.11 _____

Q.17 _____

Total _____

Charismatic – Idealized Influence

Q.1 _____

Q.13 _____

Q 20 _____

Total _____

Plot your scores

You have a total between 0 and 12 for each of the leadership styles. Please now transfer the scores above to the web below. Circle the numbers and join each of the circled numbers with a straight line.

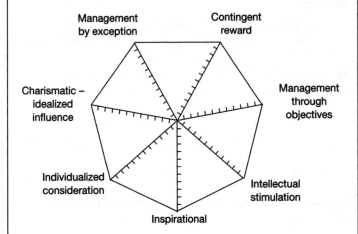

figure 1 the leadership grid

What styles do you use?

Bass identified six types of leadership style in his analysis of the 3,000 leadership studies. An additional style, Management through Objectives, is identified by Robert Dilts in *Visionary Leadership Skills*, to make the seven you work with in this book.

You have identified your perception of your strength in each style. A score of 12 means that on three behaviours that describe the style you believe that you 'frequently if not always' use that style. A score of 0 means that you believe you 'never' use that style. Note your two preferred styles, and your two least preferred styles.

Preferred   **Least Preferred**

_____   _____

_____   _____

Leadership profiles of great leaders

You may wish to compare your leadership scores, from your self-perception, to those of great leaders. Bass and Avolio used a similar assessment on 'world class' leaders using details from the leaders' biographies. The scores are adjusted to fit with the 0–12 scoring scale used in this chapter. Only five of the seven styles are considered, Inspirational and Management by Objectives were not measured. It is interesting to consider the range of styles used and the impact that these leaders had and to compare your rankings against these leaders (see Table 1).

Table 1

	Charismatic	Individualized Consideration	Intellectual Stimulation	Contingent Reward	Management by Exception
Your score					
Martin Luther King	11.7	7.5	10.2	7.2	5.7
Mahatma Gandhi	11.4	4.9	10.5	6.3	4.5
John F. Kennedy	10.6	9.3	10.2	6.0	4.7
Abraham Lincoln	8.7	7.8	8.7	5.7	6.0
Adolf Hitler	10.2	3.0	6.0	5.7	6.3
Joseph Stalin	7.1	6.3	7.2	5.7	6.9

Exercise

To consolidate your views on your styles, read the descriptions of each style in Table 2. The left-hand column describes what the style is like; the right hand describes how leaders behave within that style. Read each description and decide if that is indeed your style. You may confirm your view by your judgement on how often you use the phrase or words that go with each style. This is an enjoyable exercise to reflect on how your language reflects your leadership style.

Table 2

What leaders do	How leaders speak and act
Management by Exception Only intervene when the outcome will not be reached. Then give negative feedback and implement corrective action.	Your behaviour: Check if objectives have been reached, and take no action if everything is on course. See little need for praise or guidance. You would say: 'No news is good news.' 'I don't like that …' 'Are we reaching the objective?' Followers find acceptable behaviour by accident.
Contingent Reward Rewards are given that depend (are contingent) on behaviours displayed by the followers.	Your behaviour: Identify rewards for each follower. Negotiate rewards for success. Value incentive schemes. You would say: 'If you do X, I'll give you Y.' 'So, no X, no reward.' 'What Y do you want for doing X?'
Management through Objectives Make sure followers have agreed outcomes. Encourage followers to use their own capabilities to reach the outcomes.	Your behaviour: Work with followers to set objectives. Set up systems to measure performance against target.

Discuss what people will achieve rather than how.

You would say:
'Is your objective SMART?'
'Have you met your target?'
'If we've stated it we'll do it.'

Intellectual Stimulation

Use own ideas to compel followers to rethink their ideas. Emphasizes rational problem solving and intelligent thinking.

Your behaviour:
Challenge such thinking and stimulate alternative approaches.
Value other ideas and want to know how they would work.
Apply a rigorous analysis of the pros and cons of solutions.

You would say:
'What problems do you see?'
'What ideas do you have for solving it?'
'How else might you do that?'

Inspirational

Inspires followers through 'cheerleading'. Emphasizes values and empowering belief in future possibilities.

Your behaviour:
Encourage followers' belief in their capabilities.
Help followers to view themselves as high achievers.
Get followers to focus on what they will achieve rather than what might hold them back.

You would say:
'This is a great idea and I know we can do it.'
'There's nothing you can't achieve if you put your minds to it.'
'It will be wonderful when we do this.

Individualized Consideration

The focus is on the individual's need rather than the group's. Individual followers are supported through coaching and mentoring.

Your behaviour:
Stress the importance of the followers' values and feelings.
Can easily see problems and opportunities from others' point of view.

Readily put aside an idea and accepts others' ideas.
You would say:
'What is important to you about this?'
'Your views are really, really important to me so we can succeed.'
'Let me consider this from your position ...'

Charismatic – Idealized Influence

There is a clear mission and vision that provides a source of purpose for followers, a world is created to which followers want to belong. Followers trust and respect the leader and act towards the mission.

Your behaviour:
When you present an idea, followers imagine achieving it!
Followers act without hesitation on your idea.
Followers respect and trust your judgement and action.

You would say:
'I've had an idea that we can carry out ...'
'I have a dream for us.'
'I will never let you down.'

You will have had scores in more than one style. Consider whether your initial rankings remain the same as your understanding of the seven styles increases. As you read on and see how Ernest Shackleton used these leadership styles in his Antarctic Expedition in 1914–16, notice how he used all the seven styles to different degrees at different times.

Case analysis: Ernest Shackleton and *Endurance*

Shackleton used all seven leadership styles in the survival of the 27 men in the *Endurance* expedition of 1914–16 in Antarctica. This case analysis is based on the historically accurate British film *Shackleton* starring Kenneth Branagh that was based on Shackleton's own book *South*. Purchase details are given in the 'Taking it further' section at the end of the book – it is an excellent movie that you may now view at another level. The examples in words taken from the script, come more to life when you see the amazing beauty and inhospitality of the Antarctic landscape.

The stages in the expedition were:

December 1913	Shackleton announces expedition and begins to raise funds.
August 1914	*Endurance* leaves for Buenos Aires.
October 1914	*Endurance* leaves for Antarctica, stopping in whaling station in South Georgia.
January 1915	*Endurance* frozen in ice.
October 1915	*Endurance* crushed by ice and abandoned. Crew now living on moving ice floes.
April 1916	Set sail in three small boats.
April 1916	Arrives in Elephant Island, travelling 600 miles in seven days.
April 1916	'Greatest boat journey ever' begins with five men –17 days in storms covering over 800 miles.
May 1916	Wrecked on South Georgia.
May 1916	36-hour walk across uncharted mountains of South Georgia to whaling station.
August 1916	Returns after four attempts to pick up men in South Georgia.
	ALL SURVIVE.

Shackleton uses all seven styles *when needed*.

Management by Exception

Shackleton felt confident in the ability of his followers to complete the task. He appoints a Captain, Frank Worsley, and leaves him to sail the *Endurance* to Buenos Aries. When Shackleton arrives in Buenos Aries he inspects the ship. He discovers the Captain does not exercise sufficient discipline with the men. They have given the Captain the silly nickname 'Wozzel'. He tells Captain Wozzel that he (Shackleton) will now be in charge. Shackleton also finds on his inspection the cook is drunk and he is immediately paid off.

Thus, Shackleton only dealt with those factors that are out of line. He did not make decisions without analysis however, as he spent several days checking what had happened on board before he went aboard.

Contingent Reward

Shackleton created rewards for appropriate behaviour. When he is fund raising for the expedition, he makes it clear that the land will be named after sponsors. He asks, 'What shall we call it, this new land we have discovered?' His second-in-command, Wild, replies 'Archibald Dexter land', and 'Mount Jack Morgan'.

Shackleton needs to secure the services of Hurley as photographer to the expedition. After telling Hurley strongly that he cannot give him his expected 25 per cent of the rights, Hurley prepares to leave the ship. Shackleton intercepts him, asks for Hurley's hand, and states, '25 per cent – wasn't it?' Hurley stays. To secure the blessing of his wife, Emily, for his 'last' expedition, Shackleton proclaims 'one more trip south. That's all it will be ... I'll be too old to go again after that anyway. I'll stay at home. I'll never take my slippers off. You can nail them to my bed. I promise.'

Management through Objectives

Shackleton at times made sure that followers had agreed objectives although it is not a strongly used style. The prime example is when he set goals for survival. His followers are prepared to haul the boats (20-foot cutters) over the ice, and all set goals together – Shackleton declares 'Robertson Island', the followers respond 'Robertson Island'; Shackleton declares 'five miles a day!', the men respond 'five miles a day'.

Intellectual Stimulation

Shackleton had an awkward follower in McNish, the ship's carpenter. McNish would often question the rational problem solving and intelligence of Shackleton's decisions. When Shackleton wanted McNish to make one of the cutters watertight he posed the question to him.

Shackleton: 'I suppose there's no way we can make the Caird [a cutter] more seaworthy without the wood?'

McNish: 'Who says we don't have wood? What do you want to do?'

Shackleton: 'Make her unsinkable.'

McNish: 'Cover her over you mean? Make a deck?'
Shackleton: 'Yes, but I suppose that's impossible?'
McNish: 'Who's the carpenter around here – you or me?'

And McNish did an incredible job with limited resources.

On another occasion Shackleton needs McNish to complete two tasks. He simply poses two problems. 'It's getting a little fresh up here [on deck]. Can you do something about it?' McNish responds 'I can make a windbreak, sir'. Shackleton then poses the need 'it may be helpful to have some way of visually signalling the helmsmen now we're at the ice'. McNish replies 'Aye aye, sir.' Shackleton turns to Frank Wild, his second-in-command, and whispers 'as long as you never actually give him the solution.'

Inspirational

The use of 'cheerleading' focuses on values and beliefs. When they are about to take the boats across the ice floes Shackleton quotes from Browning – 'For sudden the worst turns the best to the brave' – and asks, 'let's make this our best'. He inspires the belief that they all will be saved as he states: 'My job now is to make sure you all live. Every single one of you. To do that I cannot afford to be sentimental. If I am, you will die. Die frozen, die starving, die mad. I've seen it all before. I do not intend to see it again.'

On another occasion Shackleton turns to the followers in a moment of crisis and tells them, 'I can honestly say there is no finer group of men'.

His speech to the complete crew as they leave Buenos Aires for the voyage is truly inspirational:

'We are learning now to carry on our white warfare. And our last message to our country is that we will do our best to make good. Though we shall be shut off from the outer world for many months our prayers and thoughts will be with our countrymen fighting at the front. We hope, in our small way, to add victories in science and discovery to that certain victory our nation shall achieve in the course of honour and liberty. Let the toast be: to victory.'

Shackleton, Buenos Aires, 26 October 1914

Individual Consideration

Shackleton would take individuals aside, and coach and mentor them through issues that affected them. He followed crew member Marston on deck. Marston had fled the Christmas celebration with a note in hand from his daughter. Shackleton asked him 'from your family?' Marston, upset, told Shackleton he was fine and to rejoin the others – Shackleton's subsequent responses are all aimed at building up Marston's confidence, and to move him back into the team as follows:

Shackleton: 'I know, I'm fine too. I just needed a little air. Such a beautiful day. Do you notice anything?'

Marston: 'What do you mean?'

Shackleton: 'Temperature's rising. We'll get there, you know.'

Marston: 'I know.'

Shackleton: 'Less than 500 miles. We're halfway. Skipper reckons we'll be inside the Antarctic Circle by tomorrow.'

Marston: 'I know.'

Shackleton: 'You don't, by any chance, have a light do you?' (as he holds up a cigar)

Marston: 'No.'

Shackleton: 'Well, come on then, let's go and find one.'

And a revived Marston rejoins the group.

On another occasion he takes Hurley, the photographer, aside to discuss why he had not chosen him to sail to South Georgia to the whaling station. He informs him that he'd 'like to have taken him, but it was right that you [Hurley] stay with the expedition. In some ways you are the expedition, your photographs will tell our story.'

Charismatic – Idealised Influence

When fund raising Shackleton creates a mission and source of purpose for his followers when he asks potential funders to:

'Close your eyes for a moment, please, and imagine Antarctica. Let your mind wander across a frozen sea, waves twisted into fantastical shapes. Icebergs like family castles shimmering in pearly shades of cobalt blue and rose. And silence. Utter. Absolute. Broken only by the thundercrack of splitting ice. The last page of that great atlas, drawn by explorers of the ancient world, lies open before us.'

And he then combines styles to use his Contingent Reward style as you've read – he asked, 'What shall we call it, this new land we have just discovered?'

The nature of leadership

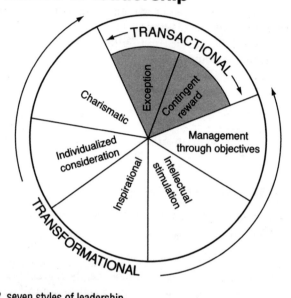

figure 2 seven styles of leadership

All of the seven leadership styles you have considered can be put into two categories, **transactional** and **transformational leadership**. You did not consider a third category, *laissez-faire*, that is the 'do-nothing', or 'leave well alone' approach. As such it is a non-leadership style. Indira Gandhi, prime minister of India (1966–77 and 1980–84) has been accused of being too *laissez-faire* in that she lacked the ability to react to avoid food crises and political instability. One of her critics said 'my impression is that one of her favourite methods of dealing with issues has been to put them on the shelf and let them be forgotten for a while and let events find their own solution.'

Transactional leadership

'If you scratch my back, I'll scratch yours.'

(anon)

The common elements in transactional leadership are that the leader:

- Uses influence to encourage and support to develop a *relationship* with the followers
- Focuses on the outcomes and on the *tasks* that are the steps towards the outcomes.

Transactional leadership styles are Management by Exception and Contingent Reward.

There are many transactional models that you may have encountered before. Examples are Hersey and Blanchard's Situational Leadership, and Blake and Mouton's Management Grid.

Transformational leadership

'Leadership is creating a world to which other people want to belong.'

Gilles Pajou

Transformational leaders have two common elements – the leader focuses attention on the *vision*, the image of the future outcomes, and attends to *actions*, the behaviours that move the leader and followers towards the outcomes.

The leader must attend to both. As Dilts points out 'vision without action is just a dream and action without vision is meaningless and boring'. Transformational styles include Management through Objectives, Intellectual Stimulation, Inspirational, Individual Consideration, Charismatic (Idealized Influence).

Which to choose?

The transformational styles are generally seen as more powerful in any given context. The more 'vision' and relevant action followers perceive, the more likely they are to act in a manner that actively supports the outcome. When transactional methods are used, there is less impact. The view that transformational styles are more powerful than transactional styles misses a key point; you need to be *flexible* in your response to differing

Table 3

Context	Leadership style
A team functions well. It typically produces good results and responds imaginatively and quickly to external change.	**Management by Exception** Leave them alone: any intervention may stunt their creativity.
There is a need to introduce a new production system over a week. The staff are unhappy about working over the weekend.	**Contingent Reward** Offer (a) triple-time pay or (b) 2 days' leave for each day worked
A new leader has taken charge of a leisure complex. There appears to be lots of activity with little direction.	**Management through Objectives** Work with the staff to set well-formed outcomes for each programme in Wet, Dry and Personal Fitness areas. Once they agree the objectives, give them space to use their own skills and capabilities.
A new leader wishes to improve the performance of his school. He has a good young staff that is bright but they seem stuck and unable to come up with ideas and solutions.	**Intellectual Stimulation** Set up and work with focus group on key issues. Introduce creative brain storming and analytical problem-solving techniques. Support them in their solutions.
A consulting organization has a very successful team that offers a well-branded standard training programme. One of the best trainers is to leave.	**Individualized Consideration** Discuss with the trainer their concerns about the programme, see the issues from their position, find out what's important to each of them and be open to accepting their solution rather than your own.

	Inspirational
A product launch had just failed. The team had been previously very successful. They have just come up with what appears to be a great idea of the same standard of their many previous successes but they seem to lack confidence to make it work this time.	Tell them how 'good' he is, how many successes he had in the past – and how wonderful it will be when the product is launched successfully.
	Charismatic – Idealized Influence
Two different departments in the public sector have been required to merge. There is a need to create a new sense of identity to allow the two groups	You create a compelling vision of a world to which both groups want to belong. Present the vision consistently and with passion – and reassure them that they have your full support.

contexts. You need differing styles for different contexts, a viewpoint that is often lost in the fruitless search for the 'right' style. As a leader, all of the styles may be appropriate in differing contexts. Examples of response of differing styles by context are given in Table 3.

Different leadership styles are required at different times. Dilts advocates this approach in the utilization of the seven leadership styles, as follows:

The leader begins by presenting the **compelling vision** to create idealized influence, then moves to **Inspiration**, the process that connects beliefs and values to the vision. **Individualized consideration** connects to the belief and value of the followers. **Intellectual stimulation** helps the followers understand how the vision can be turned into reality through action. **Contingent rewards** and **management through objectives** provide the structure and system to maintain the effort and action towards the vision. If the effort and action are maintained through time, by the followers, the leader can move towards **management by exception** as the followers take responsibility for their own action.

Others' views of your leadership style

In his original work, and in the determination of the scores for the historical characters, Bass bases the styles on the view of followers, rather than self-perception. Behind this view is, for example, that charisma is not something a leader has in themselves, rather it is a characteristic that the followers grant you. One follower may see J.F. Kennedy as charismatic. Another person may reflect on some of JFK's characteristics and not view him as charismatic.

The next exercise is to score the questionnaire below. It is worded in such a way for a 'follower' to score it for you.

How you can use the 'follower' questionnaire is described by Arthur's experience. On a leadership development seminar, Arthur, a general manager, completed the self-assessment exercise. The results confirmed his view that he had been using a style that was heavily dependent on intellectual stimulation and inspirational and management objectives to drive through change. He had moved away from using management by exception and contingency management.

Arthur decided to check his perceptions. He issued the 'Leadership Style – Others' questionnaire to his staff and he received returns from 75 per cent. His results confirmed his perception. They perceived him as using his new found charismatic and individualised consideration styles, and not management by exception and contingent reward. He was pleased that his behaviour change had been noticed. However, there was an interesting 'sting in the tail' to his results. When he discussed the results with staff, they made it clear that they needed more from him in the styles of management by exception, and contingent reward. He was perceived as not keeping his eyes on what was happening and not rewarding people. He realized that in his urge to develop new styles he had forgotten to use the other styles that his followers appreciated.

If you wish to complete the questionnaire now rather than distribute it to others, complete it as if you are your follower. Stand in their shoes, see how you are from their perspective, hear how you sound to them and feel how you feel from their perspective. You can get an even greater sense of what they are sensing by adopting their body posture. (The ability to see things from different perspectives is further discussed in Chapter 6.)

EXERCISE: Leadership Styles – Others

What is your current view of _____'s leadership style?

Listed below are some statements about leadership behaviour. Indicate how often [NAME] _____ engages in the behaviours, using the scale below to respond to each statement. Please place a number from 0 to 4 in the space beside each question.

The numbers 0 to 4 have the following meaning:

0 = never
1 = hardly ever
2 = sometimes
3 = fairly often
4 = frequently, if not always

1 _____ gives a clear vision of what we need to accomplish.

2 _____ provides followers with a clear view of the goals we want to achieve.

3 _____ inspires others by focusing on the values and beliefs of the team.

4 _____ puts forward ideas that challenge his/her follower's ideas to provide them with the stimulation to change.

5 _____ intervenes only when there is a problem.

6 _____ gives his/her followers a reward when they succeed.

7 _____ coaches each follower to succeed.

8 _____ only changes things when they go wrong.

9 _____ acts as the 'motivator' for his/her team.

10 _____ makes it clear to his/her followers what they have to do to be rewarded.

11 _____ mentors each follower.

12 _____ allows his/her followers to decide how to reach their goals.

13 _____ is viewed as someone who others wish to follow.

14 _____ helps his/her followers to look at their problems differently to provide resourceful choices.

15 _____ provides his/her followers with the opportunity to do their best.

16 _____ gives rewards and promotions for excellent performance.

17 _____ advises each follower.

18 _____ makes sure followers know when they have achieved their goals.

19 _____ encourages rational problem solving.

20 _____ believes he/she has gained the respect and trust of his/her followers.

21 _____ makes sure followers have evidence of goal achievement.

Scoring

Please now transfer your responses above to the scoring sheet below, which has three questions for each of seven leadership styles. These scores will give your impression of _____'s leadership style. Total your results.

Management by Exception	**Contingent Reward**
Q.5 _____	Q.6 _____
Q.8 _____	Q.10 _____
Q.18 _____	Q.16 _____
Total _____	Total _____

Management through Objectives	**Intellectual Stimulation**
Q.2 _____	Q.4 _____
Q.12 _____	Q.14 _____
Q.21 _____	Q.19 _____
Total _____	Total _____

Inspirational	**Individualized Consideration**
Q.3 _____	Q. 7 _____
Q.9 _____	Q.11 _____
Q.15 _____	Q.17 _____
Total _____	Total _____

Charismatic – Idealized Influence

Q.1 _____

Q.13 _____

Q 20 _____

Total _____

Plot the scores

You have a total between 0 and 12 for each of the leadership styles. Please now transfer the scores above to the web below. As before circle the numbers and join each of the circled numbers with a straight line.

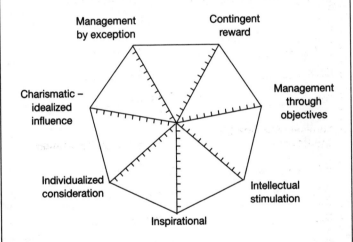

figure 3 the leadership grid

Final exercise

When you get the questionnaire back from others (or have completed it as if you were them) compare your scores from your self perception to the perception of your followers. You will gain additional insight into the perception of your leadership style. There will be confirmation of existing style choice and also gaps in perception where you believe you rate highly and your followers disagree, and vice versa.

Learning for leadership success

You have explored seven styles that leaders use – and discussed when they are appropriate to use. You have also explored your – and others' – perceptions of your preferences for each style. In the completion of the exercises you have gained a greater understanding of your preferences. A key learning point has been that you have understood the need for flexibility in your leadership approaches.

- You have understood the meaning of the following seven styles of leadership
  - Management by Exception
  - Contingent Reward
  - Management through Objectives
  - Intellectual Stimulation
  - Inspirational
  - Individualized Consideration
  - Charismatic – Idealized Influence
- You have a well-grounded perception of your preferred style
- You can recognize when different styles are appropriate
- You know that you need to be flexible – to adopt different styles at different times

You now have a clear understanding of the 'What' of leadership – the seven styles. You now know what you can change to be an effective leader. The next chapter gives you the 'How' of leadership, based on modelling how successful leaders act. The leaders come from business, public service and the community. At every level of an organization or group, and in every part of community, you can be a leader, if you choose to be one. *If one can, anyone can.*

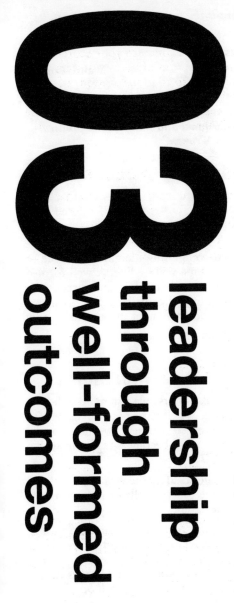

03

leadership through well-formed outcomes

In this chapter you will:
- see how powerful outcomes can focus thinking
- follow how Christabel Pankhurst, as a leader of social change, might have created her Well-Formed Outcome
- understand the technique for well-formed outcomes
- draft your own well-formed outcome for a leadership challenge you face

'Knowing what you want is the hard part, not getting it.'

Shackleton

'If you dream it, you can do it'.

Walt Disney

'Winning starts with beginning.'

Anon

'We are resolved that 1909 must and shall see the political enfranchisement of British Women.'

Christabel Pankhurst

Introduction

Leaders who lead effectively do so by recognizing that their idea needs to be compelling to others. Those leaders with the strongest sense of their own compelling idea are best able to describe what the goal or outcome will be like. A well-formed outcome allows followers to align themselves and direct their own actions towards believing in and contributing to achieving the same outcome. Bad ideas poorly thought through and badly described never succeed.

The 'voice' of Christabel Pankhurst

Using the voice of Christabel Pankhurst we can analyse how a well-formed outcome is created. Whether or not you agree with the movement that gave votes to women, wouldn't it be rewarding if you could see your ideas become a reality in such a powerful way as Pankhurst did?

On 18 December 1908, a few hours after she was released from Holloway Prison following one of her spells of imprisonment there, Christabel Pankhurst declared:

> 'The militant suffragettes who form the Women's Social and Political Union are engaged in the attempt to win the parliamentary vote for the women of this Country. Their claim is that those women who pay rates and taxes and fulfil the same qualification as men voters shall be placed upon the parliamentary register. The reasons why women should have the vote are obvious to every fair-minded person. The British constitution provides that taxation and representation shall go together, therefore women

taxpayers are entitled to vote. Parliament deals with questions of vital interest to women, such as the education, housing and employment questions and upon such matters women wish to express their opinions at the ballot box. The honour and safety of the country are in the hands of parliament; therefore every patriotic and public-spirited woman wishes to take part in controlling the actions of our legislators. We are resolved that 1909 must and shall see the political enfranchisement of British women.'

Christabel Pankhurst shows in this speech the elements of a compelling vision using a well-formed outcome.

To begin with, her stated outcome is described in the positive – *'women who pay rates and taxes and fulfill the same qualification as men voters shall be placed upon the parliamentary register.'* She does not state what is not wanted, i.e. 'we don't want women discriminated against'. The reason for stating an outcome in the positive is because the brain has the ability to focus and create its own representations – the brain has the ability to fix on a desired outcome and create its own image. It is these internal representations in the brain that make an idea able to be grasped, and once grasped, committed to. Equally, the brain is able to fix on an undesired outcome with correspondingly negative results.

Here is a story from the role of parent. One of us (Catherine) as a mother has decided that her son David is old enough to take the trainer wheels off his bicycle and ride unaided. In order to make sure he is safe they go to a quiet street where her friend Jac lives with his son Jake.

Catherine says: 'Don't be worried David by the bike being really unsteady when the trainer wheels are off; it will be a bit scary, but don't be too frightened'; 'whatever you do, don't go over near the edge of the road where it is rocky and rough'; 'and don't wobble the handle bars'; 'and whatever you do, don't turn around and look at me.'

While reading this transcript you are likely to have made a kind of mini-movie in your head of David riding to the edge of the road, wobbling his handle bars, turning his head around to look at his mother and then falling off complete with wailing. And this is exactly what did happen – 'Mum, I can't do this – I hate you.' David's brain, like yours, needs to create sensory representations, pictures, sounds and feelings of what it is being asked to think about. In this case it was being asked to think about what it was not to do. The brain really can't cope with the idea of the word 'don't'

So Jac then asked David to: 'have another go and this time keep your eyes on the middle of the road'; 'lift your head up and pedal evenly'; 'enjoy yourself.' The brain also creates sensory representations, pictures, sounds, and feelings of what it is being asked to think about and this time David rode quite some way without falling and even when he did came racing back full of enthusiasm to have another turn and get it right.

So being able to describe what you *do* want rather than what you *don't* want will increase your chances of getting your outcomes achieved.

A statement of what one wants to be moving towards (the desirable outcome), rather than moving away from (the undesirable outcome), permits alignment of stated intentions and actions.

Other effective leaders also use visionary images:

> *'I see one nation, one people. Then I see us dealing with the economic situation.'*
>
> Nelson Mandela, when in prison

> *'And so, my fellow Americans: ask not what your country can do for you – ask what you can do for your country. My fellow citizens of the world: ask not what America will do for you, but what together we can do for the freedom of man.'*
>
> John F. Kennedy, Inaugural address, 20 January 1961

> *'I have a dream that one day this nation will rise up, live out the true meaning of its creed: we hold these truths to be self evident, that all men are created equal.'*
>
> Reverend Martin Luther King, Washington,
> 27 August 1963

> *'We know how rough the road will be, how heavy here the load will be; we know about the barricades that wait along the track, but we have set our soul ahead upon a certain goal ahead and nothing left, from hell to sky shall ever turn us back.*
>
> Vince Lombardi, American football coach

We will now describe the seven steps that lead to a well-formed outcome with examples from Christabel Pankhurst.

Seven steps for a well-formed outcome

1 State outcomes in the positive

Leaders who regularly achieve what they want are proactive or visionary in their thinking. They are firmly focused in the future, can describe their outcome and therefore are able to move towards the outcome and often achieve it.

Pankhurst's commitment to the future is evident in her words, 'We are resolved that 1909 must and shall see the political enfranchisement of British women.' She also uses compelling language to describe the outcome. Imagine the people outside the prison gate. The audience is bathed in the belief. As she describes the outcome compellingly, they absorb that belief there and then. Her vision is made richer by her references to 'women who pay rates and taxes', 'every fair-minded person', 'British constitution provides that taxation and representation shall go together', 'Parliament deals with questions of vital interest to women', and 'the honour and safety of the country'. As you read Christabel's declaration (on pages 34–35) you may have created a picture of the people at the gate, simulated or recalled their voices and have had a sense of the excitement, power and emotion her statement would have created for you if you had been there.

Thus, **stating your outcome in a positive way** is the first step to a well-formed outcome.

2 Sensory specific

When you **state what you will see, hear and feel** in such a sensory specific way, you help to associate the listener (and yourself) with the experience and to test for himself whether it is something he wants to have for real. The more compelling the description is, the more committed the listener will become, such as: '*We will see women at the ballot box, hear people claiming their right to vote, and feel proud of the way we can shape the future in this country.*'

3 Context

In this example Christabel's objective is framed within the **context** of the contemporary political environment. The context within the well-formed outcome technique is an important factor and is defined as when and where the outcome is to take place and who else will be there. It sets the scope. You know the scale that you are talking about. Knowing and describing the context specifically makes the definition even clearer. In this case she is only asking for votes for women who pay taxes as only men who paid taxes had the vote at that time. She is asking for the possible dream of suffrage on the same terms as men. Her vision is firmly set in the political and social context of 1908. She does not, at this stage, ask for universal suffrage, votes for all regardless of status.

4 Fit and ecology

So how does this fit? How does Christabel's idea of women's suffrage fit with the rest of her life? We already know that she is willing to go to prison in pursuit of her outcome. Her actions will have had negative consequences for herself and her family, such as bringing shame to some members of her family. Leadership of change doesn't come without its consequences, positive and negative. Your life has a certain ecology – how is this ecology affected by the actions you propose to take. To understand what leading will do for you, it is necessary to understand what else will have to change in order to allow it to happen, what and who else will have to shift to fit in with the new reality that is envisaged and what physical resources are needed to achieve the outcome.

What could stop you? Leaders think about what holds back change. Christabel Pankhurst has taken a courageous stance, which has involved her being imprisoned. What is it in the present that is resistant to change? If you can be stopped, then the goal is not yet well formed and may be unachievable. So work through the question 'What would it take to overcome this?'

The notion of **secondary gain** may explain why women before her were held back from taking actions such as Pankhurst's. Secondary gain is the benefit that inaction or current actions give you. For example, if Christabel Pankhurst had not pursued suffrage for women she would have been able to live a privileged and settled lifestyle of the Edwardian lady. It is interesting to speculate whether the conversation at the dinner table of the Pankhurst family ever considered the advantages (the secondary gain) of her not pursuing the outcome. Therefore, the question to ask is 'What will be even better in the desired future so that it is possible willingly to let go of current gains in order to move to the even better future?'

5 What are the resources needed?

One step towards a well-formed outcome is to check whether you have the resources you can activate to get your outcome. For Christabel Pankhurst internal resources may have been what we would call courage and tenacity. She may have needed funding from others and she would have needed the internal resource of being able to influence and negotiate to get it. She also had the self belief that what she could do would have an effect and that she was able to do something today and that she could continue to do it. She could envisage a sustained effort on her part that would get her to her final goal. Her actions would imply that there was nothing in the world that was going to stop her. Had she been proposing her actions in 1914, the greater need for unity in the First World War may have rendered her message unheard. Indeed during the war (1914 to 1918) the Pankhurst family suspended their campaign and committed themselves to charitable work to support the war effort. So you see she also had the internal resource of judgement and timing.

6 Check if your outcome is still desirable

To achieve the outcome will take commitment and enthusiasm. Before you start, cross-check that the efforts you will put in are worth the rewards of achieving your outcome. It is better to have let go of an idea you have thought through and no longer wish to pursue than it is to drive on with an idea that is ill conceived.

7 Commit to the first step

Having made the desirability of the outcome clear and checked for desirability, another characteristic of the leader is that when the outcome is compelling they then take action. They not only know the first step towards their outcome, they take it. Christabel Pankhurst makes her speech in the middle of the campaign. She had already taken the first step.

A well-formed outcome, which is compelling at one time, can change. We know that the Pankhursts were flexible in terms of the actions they took during the First World War. It also may have been that the discussions around the Edwardian table about the outcome may have moved from the more liberal but inconceivable concept of universal suffrage for men and women to the more conceivable one of votes for the taxpayers.

Flexibility to adjust the outcome can be supported if the overarching outcome remains clear. The outcome may not be achieved without hiccups or changes and alterations, and the clarity of the image of the outcome is the magnetic pull that will guide great leaders, and you, towards achieving their goals.

'It is a mistake to look too far ahead. Only one link in the chain of destiny can be handled at a time.'

Winston Churchill

Figure 4 is a model of the well-formed outcome technique.

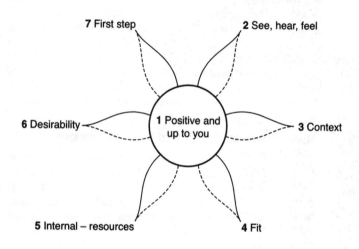

Figure 4 well-formed outcome

04

the building blocks of leadership

In this chapter you will:

- understand what makes us believe the techniques in this book work, our *presuppositions*
- use the *three-minute leadership seminar*
- develop your *awareness* so you know better how your leadership is going
- be able to build *rapport* in a powerful and easy way
- learn how to *learn* more effectively – for yourself and others

'Excellence is not an act but a habit.'
Aristotle

Introduction

In Chapter 2 we introduced differing views on leadership and in Chapter 3 you developed your own *well-formed outcome*. You now know the outcome you want to achieve as a leader, so this and the next chapters will tell you **how** to achieve. The 'how' comes from an analysis of high performing leaders – their behaviours, programmes, patterns and beliefs in self-leadership and the leadership of others.

There are many approaches that aim to improve the leader's potential and performance. You may have tried some – visualization, affirmations, goal setting – and with differing degrees of success. Sometimes the techniques work and sometimes they don't. And yet you still want to develop and achieve high performance. The techniques below will give you the key to a level of *consistent high performance* in your leadership actions.

What presupposes us to believe the techniques work?

Organizations that model what other organizations do and then adapt it for their own use call it 'best practice'. Rank Xerox and Motorola have successfully used best practice to improve their productivity. The incredible resurgence of Japan's manufacturing in the 1950s and beyond was based on modelling best practice quality processes. And in the 1970s Western organizations then modelled themselves on the Japanese 'best practice'! The techniques we explore are developed from modelling high performers and great leaders; for example, Winston Churchill, Ernest Shackleton, Mahatma Gandhi, Martin Luther King, Abraham Lincoln, John F. Kennedy. And also from the many leaders in organizations we have met who have given us examples of excellent leadership practice on a smaller scale.

The following ideas are the bedrock that form the sound foundations for the remaining chapters. By understanding these ideas you will have maximum gain from what follows. Our belief is that these ideas are valuable because of our success in using them with leaders in our development and coaching practice. As the ideas work for us, and for others with whom we work, we have real confidence in recommending them for you.

If one can, anyone can

In the 1950s it was a common belief that man could not run a mile in less than four minutes. Roger Bannister did not hold this belief and he broke the four minute barrier. Once broken, others found the inner belief to break the four minute barrier over and over again. 'If Bannister can, I can'. Never underestimate the power of 'I can'. The choice is yours – we believe all people have the necessary resources to make any change they really want. Nothing in this book is as difficult as learning a language. With few exceptions all of us can speak our native tongue. Many choose not to learn a second language – despite the efforts of the education system. Yet many do learn two, three or more languages because they choose to and because they choose, they can.

There is no failure, only feedback

'I choose life over death … and if I should fail, then I will try again. The only true failure would be not to explore at all.'

Shackleton

If you do not achieve the outcome you want, do something else and persist. You use feedback to discover what you need to change to succeed, and keep changing until you achieve what you want.

Thinking of failure is not helpful. If we fail at one thing and focus on the failure it is but a small step to believe we are failures … and if we fail a few times, and keep focusing on what isn't working we create a self-fulfilling prophecy that we are a 'total' failure in all things. Our energy flows where attention goes. The remarkable results that are achieved by dedicated teachers in so-called 'failing schools' are often based on creating success in small matters with the kids that turn into a big success overall.

The following is a short biography. Who is it describing?

Failed in business at age 31
Defeated in a legislative race at 32
Failed in business at 34
Nervous breakdown at age 36

Lost election at age 38
Lost congressional race at age 46
Lost congressional race at age 48
Lost senatorial race at age 55
Lost Vice Presidential race at age 56
Lost senatorial race at age 58
Elected president at age 60

The leader was Abraham Lincoln. He learned from every failure and became a President who kept the Union intact in the United States.

The leader with the most flexibility will control the system

Leaders who succeed display flexibility in their behaviour. They change what they do – and thus the response they get – as outside factors change. Leaders who do not succeed in the long term, though they may in the short term, maintain a consistent pattern of behaviour. Margaret Thatcher was successful using a domineering authoritarian style. Times changed, and the country and her followers required a different style. She did not believe it necessary, or chose not, to change. She was unceremoniously dropped by her senior colleagues and the Party.

Leaders who do not wish to change, who are inflexible, will state that the system and/or others need to change. Flexible leaders change themselves and thus change the response they get from others.

Fiedler's leadership theory, Leader–Match, is the only theory that assumes leaders cannot change. In this theory the leader therefore must analyse the leadership situation, by means of an analytical tool, and move to the situation that suits. In the natural world this belief does not hold. Animals that succeed are those that adapt to the changing world. Many animal species such as foxes have adapted to the urban world. Our belief is that individuals can choose, and by changing flexibly your own behaviour to what is required in the situation you can be effective – if you choose to be.

If you always do what you have always done you always get what you have always got

Effective leaders learn from their experience, and if what they are doing does not work, do something else – that moves them towards their outcome. Shackleton in dealing with a crisis was a master of being flexible and changing what was happening. Within four days on the trip towards Elephant Island he changed his plans – first from heading towards Elephant Island to the east, to aiming for King George Island to the west, to trying for Hope Bay to the south west, and back to Elephant Island. The effective leader recognizes that persisting with old behaviour gets them nowhere – except for the place they do not want to be!

We learn in small ways too. The other day a colleague was driving the route she always took through the lanes and winding roads to avoid the motorways. She reckoned this was the best route to work. There was an accident ahead and faced with waiting many minutes, or opting for a different route, she consulted the map and found an even better short cut to her destination. We wonder how long she would have just kept going the same way because she 'always did it that way'?

I'm in charge of my mind and therefore my behaviour

The final presupposition we wish to share – a belief that affects the way you behave – in this section is one which gives you the confidence that you will be able to successfully implement the learning that follows, to understand what is said and be able to make whatever changes you need to in your behaviour.

You *can* make the changes that you need to. In Chapter 3 we showed how the mind, body and behaviour are related in one system in creating a well-formed outcome. Thus if you choose to do something (in your mind) your behaviour will follow.

Many people act as if they are not in charge. It's other people who make them do things or make things happen to them. It's always someone or something else's fault.

It's hard to imagine but it is as if Nelson Mandela sat in Robbin's Island and said 'There's nothing I can do, the forces of apartheid are too strong'; or Abraham Lincoln sat in the White House and stated that 'We can't do anything about slavery. It's better just to split the country in two'; or William Wilberforce, who campaigned for abolition of slavery in the British Empire, said 'the economic forces that make slavery inevitable are too strong'.

If these great leaders had made these statements, they would have been at **effect**. They would have been made powerless by others. Instead they were at **cause**. Each believed they could cause things to change, and they did using all of the techniques that follow. You have read five of the presuppositions of effective leadership here. You will meet others later in the text.

The three-minute leadership seminar

The short version of the key to effective leadership is that if we wish to be effective leaders we should:

- Have a very clear notion of the outcome we want to achieve and keep it in focus, a well-formed outcome
- Be aware and alert so we notice how we move towards the outcome
- Have the flexibility to change what we do, and keep changing until the outcome is achieved.

In short the three keys to effective leadership are:

OUTCOME
AWARENESS
FLEXIBILITY

Flexibility is the first skill for knowing what your outcome is. If you don't know where you are going you may end up somewhere else. Bodenhamer and Hall suggest that only 5 per cent of the population in the USA have clear outcomes. While the percentage may not be entirely accurate, they make a powerful point by asking 'what do the other 95% do?' The answer is 'work for the 5%'!

You learned how to set outcomes that were compelling in Chapter 3. Set your outcome first. Be able to describe it clearly and with passion to others.

Second, is the skill of awareness – knowing where to place your attention and how to make sense of the enormous quantity of data that is available to you every day.

Thirdly, flexibility is the ability to change if your awareness indicates that you are not achieving your outcomes. You may not get straight to your outcome in the manner you first imagined. Your course may be zig-zagging and if you choose to persist and adapt to the circumstances you find you will still get to your well-formed outcome by whatever path it takes.

Awareness for leadership

The next section gives us more understanding of how effective leaders become aware, how they demonstrate high acuity skills, and how they notice what is happening as events and people move towards the outcome.

> 'The range of what we think, do, and achieve is limited by what we fail to notice. And because we fail to notice what it is that we fail to notice then there is little we can do to change ... until we notice how failing to notice shapes our thoughts and deeds.'
>
> John Grinder

Awareness is about having your antennae well tuned and being able to read the signals life is sending you.

Awareness in action

When leading a team meeting, Joyce observed the following behaviours and she made the following observations:

- George is looking down to his right, his face muscles are slack and his breathing is shallow.
- Safraz is sitting back in his chair, legs stretched out before him; hands behind his head, breathing slowly and deeply, with eyes raised.
- Bill is sitting hunched forward, arms crossed with hands tightly holding the arms. Eyes are down.

Joyce perceived their behaviours as:

- George is depressed.
- Safraz knows all the answers, he's confident and understands what's happening.
- Bill feels under threat.

How to be aware as a leader

Joyce has sensed how her followers in the meeting have responded to her leadership behaviours. She has made a judgement about the impact she has had – and has observed her followers closely and accurately. Yet her understanding may be faulty.

We could argue that the communication comes only through the words that are spoken. We might expect Bill to say 'those ideas threaten me', and Safraz to say 'I fully understand where you are going'. We must question whether George would say that he's depressed! Let us explore how these interpretations may be faulty.

Even if Bill, Safraz and George had said the words above they do not convey the full meaning. Ray Birdwhistle conducted a series of experiments at the University of Pennsylvania that conclude only 7 per cent of meaning in communication that contains an emotional element comes from words, 38 per cent from the voice and tone, and 55 per cent from the body posture and presentation (see Figure 5).

```
+-----------------------------------+
|          Words (7%)               |
+-----------------------------------+
|                                   |
|          Tone (38%)               |
|                                   |
+-----------------------------------+
|                                   |
|                                   |
|          Body                     |
|          language (55%)           |
|                                   |
|                                   |
+-----------------------------------+
```

figure 5 percentage used to make meaning of a communication

If we are to interpret accurately what is the message, the meaning of the communication, we need to pay attention to:

- *Body movements* – posture, gestures, breathing, facial expressions, eye movements, muscle and skin colour changes
- *Voice* – tones, accents, stresses, pauses, intonation, rhythm and pitch
- *Words* – the precise language used

It is an important skill of leadership to observe those around us. Fine tuning our sensory awareness means that we begin to notice more and more how people change from minute to minute. This is a key skill in more effective communication and enables us to monitor with greater accuracy what people are experiencing, and combined with other evidence may identify how a person is responding to your leadership. We can begin to recognize clusters/patterns of behaviour that give clear meaning in their messages and indeed we already read people well. A leader we know worked with a Director who gave very clear signs that he was about to lose his cool. His lips would disappear into his mouth, the muscle round the mouth would tense and the shade and shape of his eyes would change. This leader knew when to take avoiding action. Her colleagues, without the same awareness, would not. Below we consider how to develop your awareness skills in leadership. The awareness skills are a key part of influencing and communicating and will be further explored in Chapter 6.

The body

Within the 55 per cent of communication that is attributed to body there are four key areas that you may observe, if you have the awareness to do so. The main areas are body posture, gestures and movement, skin tone and texture. The signs which give the most information are:

Breathing: A person's breathing tells a great deal about them. As you notice breathing, observe whether they breathe in their chest or stomach or high up almost in their throat. It may be unacceptable to observe an individual's chest. In which case if you watch the shoulder movement you can judge breathing. Watch for patterns in how someone's breathing reflects their mood and behaviour patterns.

Colour changes: Observing colour change may seem an odd, and perhaps impossible skill. Yet it is likely that we all do it. When someone's face reddens you often make a mind read of anger, embarrassment or energy shift. There are physiological reasons why this happens that are connected with changes in the movement of blood in the veins. What is not clear is what is the meaning. There are other changes in colour that occur less often – you can see greys, blues, yellowing and changes in intensity of colouring, darkening and lightening.

Muscle changes: As colour changes, so do the muscles. The change is often around the mouth, such as a tight smile or minute grimace. Foreheads and eyes crease (and uncrease). The notion of a 'tension headache' speaks literally about this process. You can notice when people are gritting their teeth, tensing their shoulders or jiggling their keys.

Mouth changes: Observing the mouth allows us to examine changes in colour, skin tightness and lip. An interesting area as it is unlikely that the person you are observing would be able to control their movements. We can notice changes in colour, size, shape, edges, texture, and swelling.

Voice: Observing the voice can be subdivided into tone and the words used. Regarding tone, when someone says 'thank you' it can be a genuine 'thank you for your help' – or it may be a 'so thank you for giving me even more work'. The voice tone is significant in communication. Changes in the tone may signify a change in the individual. As the voice changes the individual's state will change. The changes to hear are volume, pitch, rhythms, tempo, clarity and resonance.

Words have meaning. Often the precise meaning is only held by the speaker. The listener interprets and can make an incorrect interpretation. If you are not listening to the tone the irony of the thank you can be missed. To get at the deeper meaning, you can ask, 'What specifically do you mean by?' Other examples of precision language are discussed in Chapter 6.

Voice interpretation

Let us go back to our three characters George, Safraz and Bill. The Manager, Joyce has shown good awareness skills to accurately observe her team's behaviour. What she may do is to take from the patterns an interpretation of their behaviour, a mind read. Joyce may be correct in her mind reads and she may not be. If she decided to ask Bill 'What makes you sense you are under threat?', he might respond 'I'm not, I'm just cold and I'm keeping warm'. He might also believe he's under attack and begin, 'What made you think I'm under threat? Do you think I'm incompetent and can't do the job?' What happens now is that the focus of the meeting may be lost and the focus becomes Bill – and his perception that his competence is being questioned.

Joyce should be aware of what happens to avoid coming to conclusions about people's state that lead her to use inappropriate behaviour. She would be on safer ground to ask 'I notice you sitting with your arms tightly folded – is there a reason for this?'

How to utilize the observations

We have already cautioned Joyce about rushing too quickly into judgement and taking actions with her followers. If she had been more aware she could look for patterns of behaviour. If the patterns of behaviour were repeated, she could begin to make her judgements with some reliability. If Bill repeated his behaviour of hunching with arms crossed tightly consistently, Joyce could judge that he was in the same state. If he had at some stage stated, 'This is very difficult, I'm not sure how it affects me, and appears to undermine my position', and had held the same voice and body posture she could reasonably state he believed he was under threat. Once Joyce learns to observe and recognize behaviour patterns she has much more data to act on at an early stage and thus increases the likelihood of being able to influence Bill's actions and responses.

Spotting the patterns: calibration

Joyce in this case has used her awareness skills. She can now identify Bill's state, his being under threat, even if he does not speak or before he speaks. Since people's behaviour is remarkably consistent, we can make judgements and rely on that pattern of observation. The key is that the consistency is within the individual. We cannot generalize across groups of individuals. Bill and Safraz may both be angry – Bill may demonstrate lots of movement whereas Safraz goes still. The process of identification of a state from the signals of tonality and body posture and comparing this state with people's normal state is often referred to as calibration and has three steps:

• **Look and listen** to notice consistent patterns of behaviour
• Pause, and **check your observations.** Compare with previous situations. If in doubt, wait for more information before you …
• Reach a **conclusion**

EXERCISE: How well do you spot the patterns?

You may already calibrate well. If you ask your partner 'whether they want to go out for a meal', you will probably know the answer before the words are spoken. This exercise will help you to refine your skills.

In a meeting, or at home, notice what happens in a discussion to one individual on the scale below.

Voice:	Slow	Medium	Fast
	Low	Steady	High
	Quiet	Even	Animated
Mouth skin:	Pink	Red	Pursed
	Dull	Shiny	Wrinkled
	Tight	Relaxed	Smiling
Breathing:	Chest	Even	Stomach
	Fast	Steady	Deep
Colour changes:	write down the colour changes		
	Deeper	Lighter	
	Brightness	Dull	

You may wish to practise by observing only one aspect of behaviour, e.g. voice tone. Many differences are slight and unmistakable. To look and listen for all at once may be an overload. As your senses become sharper, you will detect finer and finer changes. And you will notice other changes that may be more significant for the person you are observing. Note these down and remember.

- Look and listen to notice **consistent** patterns of behaviour, such that you begin to match the change with the consequent behaviour.
- Pause to check your observations **before** reaching a conclusion. Check that change is related to the behaviour before you make an inference and behave in a way that gets a response you did not expect or want, as happened to Joyce when she challenged Bill on his defensiveness.

Rapport

'Treat others as you want to be treated – on and off the job. Listen closely to others' concerns and show that you value them.'

Anon

Rapport is the process of establishing and maintaining a relationship between two or more people that facilitates and creates a desired response from the other person. Without rapport we cannot communicate effectively and without communication we cannot lead.

An example of this is provided by Jim when he's on the phone. He was puzzled because he frequently telephoned two colleagues and normally attained his outcome with one, but with the other always seemed to end up in an argument, the intended outcome lost. We listened to his calls on a speaker-phone to give him some feedback. But with the colleague he got on with, it was evident that both were speaking in a very similar tone of voice at about the same rate of speech, moderately fast. But with the colleague he tended to argue with, Jim spoke in a much slower tempo, using lower and softer tones compared with the rapid, high-pitched language of his colleague. So we were able to point out to Jim that the words used in each conversation were very similar, but the only major difference was voice tempo and tone.

We communicate, and thus potentially lead, all the time. Even when we do not speak we communicate non-verbally. Leaders are aware that they cannot *not* communicate. Every movement, every gesture portrays a meaning. Richard Nixon in debate with John F. Kennedy was seen to sweat profusely from his brow. Viewers mind read the beads of sweat as weaknesses, inability to cope with stress, nervousness and uncertainty. They did not wish to vote for a President with these characteristics. In contrast those listeners who heard the debate on the radio, who did not see the sweating, thought Nixon had won the debate.

What happens often in our communication is that we say one thing, but our body posture and voice 'leak' another meaning. Tony Blair gave a party conference speech that was televised. His fine words, discussed in Chapter 8, are forgotten by most. What *is* remembered is the heavy sweating in his blue shirt. This may seem a trivial example, and yet we know instinctively when someone is 'saying one thing and portraying another' – it comes across as incongruent and less believable.

If you have high level rapport skills, you can lead using the techniques in Chapters 5–8. You know when you have rapport – when you and the person you are with are on the same wavelength and ideas flow and you listen and are listened to. You can see people in rapport in many settings – bars, over dinner, in a corridor, at a meeting. And you know when people are not in rapport.

We cannot communicate effectively without rapport. If you have a relationship with someone that is comfortable and easy, both parties are more likely to listen and engage. We explore below how to make it so. If you are uneasy you are unlikely to communicate comfortably. We will show you how to build rapport to increase connection with people you want to influence. It can also be useful to help break uncomfortable communication and have a way of bringing it to an end. You may find this technique of intentionally breaking rapport particularly helpful when you are next caught in conversation with someone who is going on ... and on and on.

People can get their own way without rapport. In this case, you are not influencing, but rather may be relying on coercing and manipulating. Why influence through rapport rather than coercion and manipulation? Coercion works only when there is sufficient power in the hands of the coercer and those you coerce will endeavour to get you back. Influencing through rapport works no matter the relative power position of the influencer. Influencing through rapport takes less effort and energy than coercion. A subordinate can influence using rapport. Ability to build relationships in sales and marketing is based on rapport. People will buy from a salesperson with whom they have rapport rather than buy the better product. As you listen to why colleagues and friends purchased from a salesperson, followed a leader, listen (using your new found sensory awareness) to how often rapport, by word or by description, is mentioned.

How to build rapport

The first step in building rapport is realizing that rapport is a process.

- Rapport is a naturally occurring unconscious process between people who get on well. Learning about rapport building gives us the choice to build rapport with anyone, anytime, anywhere.
- If you operate with a win–win outcome, where both people achieve their outcome, you are likely to be able to influence over and over again.
- Knowing how to build and develop rapport allows you to break rapport – to mismatch. Knowing how to mismatch gives you more choice in interrupting a conversation with two others or being able to end a conversation with someone else.

We do things to generate rapport. It does not just happen. The key process in rapport building is **matching**. People who are in rapport tend to match or align with each other in a number of ways. In broad terms we match with all elements of communication – words, body posture and voice.

We match **words** by matching how the other person presents the words. We match on:

- Length of phrase and sentence
- Key words in phrase (including jargon)
- Common experience and memories
- How others describe their experiences – do they describe pictures, tell stories, or give feelings?

The impact of these processes is powerful. To illustrate this, it is easy to remember *mis*matching through words. For example, what were your feelings when:

- A professional, say a doctor, used key words and phrases that you don't understand and made you feel uncomfortable and stupid? It is not surprising that patients often do not take doctors' advice. Compare this experience with one where the jargon or phrases were explained in terms you could understand.

- Someone described in great detail a sporting experience that you dislike – darts, golf, skiing, Manchester United? Compare this with how you felt when someone discusses something that is a common interest. Manchester United is a very common example. It is the most anticipated football result. The minority are those United fans who want them to succeed. The majority are the ABUs (anyone but United) who want them to lose! And – May we tell you about 'the eagle at the 12th at Nairn and Portnoo Golf Club in Donegal in Summer 2000. It was 29 September and a 7 iron to ...' The golfer may be comfortable and enjoying the story and want to know 'What's next?'. The non-golfer will be switched off!

Body posture gives us many choices for matching. We can match:

- Leg positions – legs crossed, stretched out, resting on knee, desk or any other position
- Head – tilt, down, to side, up, nodding
- Breathing – through chest or stomach, speed, depth
- Movements – of hands, legs, fingers and body
- Arm position – folded (which arm is on top), close to body/wide
- Voice – tone/pitch, pace/volume, language
- Eyes – blink rate

The process of matching

When we wish to be in rapport the objective is to be similar, to mirror the other person in the categories identified above.

As we learn how matching works, pick one body match only. When the follower folds their arms, fold your arms. As we get more comfortable choose another thing to match. Match their breathing. When the breathing speed changes follow the speed ... and so on.

Always bear in mind your outcome is to build rapport. When we first try to match, we may begin to mimic, grossly following each movement. If this mimicking becomes obvious it may be insulting. Matching should be done step by step at an appropriate pace. We should never mimic (unless your outcome is to insult!). However, mirroring can be used where it is comfortable for both, and this builds rapport when it is subtle. Mirroring may have the practical disadvantage that it may move you to an uncomfortably high level of rapport.

It is possible to build too much rapport in a given context. Many years ago one of us had just learned about rapport and was in a meeting with a potential new client for his organization. After matching body movements, language and particular language and experiences, the potential client said, 'I'll be very happy to work with you, but not with your organization'. An inappropriate level of personal rapport had been built, and the outcome, work for the organization, had not been achieved. More awareness with greater calibration of what had happened in the meeting (remember there was learning and experimenting) may have led to more flexible behaviour to achieve the outcome. Too much rapport may, in a work context, make it difficult to break away. If you are a natural rapport builder it is likely that you have people coming to discuss issues more often, and in a more intimate fashion, than you may believe is appropriate. In personal relationships where you wish to be more intimate, higher levels of rapport may be useful. It is useful to think of rapport as a process where we can go to an appropriate level.

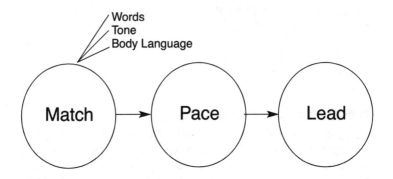

figure 6 rapport building

Rapport building

The process of using rapport contains three stages:

Matching → Pace → Lead

We begin by matching – and then pace the individual by matching until we are comfortable with a level of rapport. If we then start to change slowly what we are doing, the other person will follow. If we have good rapport we will see the other person begin to follow our changed behaviour – posture or voice. When we have matched and they have followed then we can begin to introduce the new ideas and thought pattern that we want them to follow. We can lead.

The metaphor of creating a bridge and leading over it, as shown in Figure 7, is an elegant way to summarize this concept.

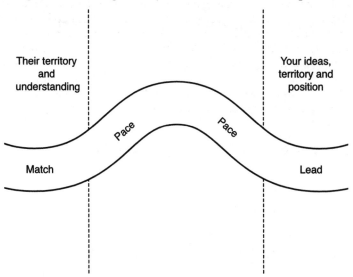

figure 7 bridge metaphor for rapport building

An excellent use of pacing and leading is when we are faced with an arguing colleague. We match the anger by possibly raising voice tone or adapting their agitated posture. We then match and pace – pace – pace – pace – until we lead them to a more amenable mood.

It is important to match their state, to show that there is respect for their position. This acknowledges their feeling about the issue without us agreeing with their point of view, e.g. 'I can see you are upset and this is important to you'. Once we have matched and paced and established rapport, we can start to lead them towards a more rational position by softening our posture and lowering our tone. We can then lead them to a position where they can consider the issue objectively, e.g. 'I agree resolution of the issue is important and what I propose we consider is …' 'Let's look at this together'.

Within a large group we can use match–pace–lead with individuals who disagree with the leader's viewpoint. They may demonstrate their lack of rapport by adopting different postures, or other differences. When we match and pace them, we can see them begin to change (using our heightened sensory awareness) and then begin to lead them towards a position where they are able to see things from our point of view.

When do we know when there is rapport?

Here are five indications of rapport:

1 Check their matching of your body posture, voice and words.
2 Notice if there is an internal feeling, say in the stomach. At first the feeling may be that of discomfort. Thereafter the feeling turns to comfort as we feel warmth of rapport with the other person.
3 Within a minute, after the warm feeling, there may be changes in the other person's colour. There may be the sensation of blushing in you.
4 There may be statements demonstrating a connectedness, e.g. 'I feel I have known you before', 'I find it so easy to talk to you'.
5 Now test rapport by leading and observe the other person following. Make the test something that you can easily notice. If we scratch an ear, they will follow. If we shift position, they will follow. If we change the subject in discussion, the other follows – Now you have rapport!

What are they seeing of you?

Experience with thousands of people who have learned rapport and the other techniques outlined in the book are that good matching is rarely noticed. Everyone else will not notice. People are so caught up in the content of their issue, that they do not observe the building of rapport in a subtle manner. And on the rare occasion when they do, if we respond to the question 'what are you doing?' with 'building rapport', it's a very acceptable activity. How can someone object to the building of rapport? We do however have one example of rapport being noticed. The two people had met rapport at identical courses one week apart. Jacqui was selling to Stanley who noticed, using his new found acuity, that Jacqui was matching. He challenged her saying 'you are using rapport. aren't you?' She said 'yes', and got the sale. Indeed, Rapport was built on the topic of Rapport!

Exercise to build rapport

You have already practised your awareness skills, so you are able to notice more easily changes in others. In this exercise you will develop your skills in matching, pacing and leading using your voice.

1 Choose an unimportant situation. Pick a context where there is little at stake, such as a meeting over coffee with a colleague or a stranger in a public place. You will learn more if the other person does not know what is happening.

2 Match their voice – its pace, volume, tone, pitch. As you talk adjust your voice until it is similar to the other's. Notice what happens to the communication – easier or more difficult? Have you a feeling of rapport?

3 Now mismatch – alter your voice so that it is different from the other's. Increase your volume, pace, tone or pitch. Notice the impact on the communication – easier or more difficult? What has happened to the feeling of rapport?

If you have quickly established rapport in stage 2, you may find a dramatic and noticeable change at stage 3 as you have taken away from the other person a good feeling, rapport, that they enjoy.

4 Now return to matching. Change back to matching volume, pace, tone or pitch and notice how the smooth flow of communication returns.

Once you have demonstrated to yourself the power of rapport in voice matching, practise on the other elements:

- Words:
  - Length of phrases and sentences
  - Key words and phrases
  - Common experience and memories
  - How people describe their experiences – pictures, stories or feelings

- Body posture:
  - Leg position
  - Head
  - Breathing
  - Movements of hands, legs, fingers etc.
  - Arm position
  - Eyes – blink rate

And as you become more expert, and matching becomes easier and easier, you will begin to combine the three elements of voice, body posture and words.

When you are comfortable with your ability to create rapport through matching and pacing, test the level of rapport by leading – in voice, body posture and language. When you have led, and the other has followed, you are now able to lead towards your leadership outcome. When you have rapport, you will be surprised how easily you can lead and others will follow.

Learning for leadership

You have been tasked with much in the last self-exercise. The key to your development is that you learn as effectively as possible. To learn these leadership skills you must understand them, and also practise them. It will help your learning if you understand how you learn. Learning is the last building block of leadership. We can also use this understanding to improve how we help others to learn.

A key to understanding the learning process is that the learning of skills is a process where we move from conscious to unconscious. As discussed further in Chapter 6, the conscious mind has a limited capacity of five to nine pieces of information. Yet when we drive a car, ride a bicycle, play a sport, or give a presentation, we demonstrate skills with many more pieces of information. To check how true this limited capacity is, think back to when we learned to drive a car or ride a bicycle. How difficult it is to change gear, use the clutch, steer the car, look in the rear mirror and so on … It's complicated, isn't it!

How we cope is by consciously mastering small pieces of skill, combining them into larger and larger chunks, until they become habitual and unconscious. When the habit is formed we are free to notice other things.

The stages of learning follow the four stages from unconscious incompetence to unconscious competence as shown in Figure 8. As we practise our awareness, or rapport skills, we may go through these stages, at varying speeds.

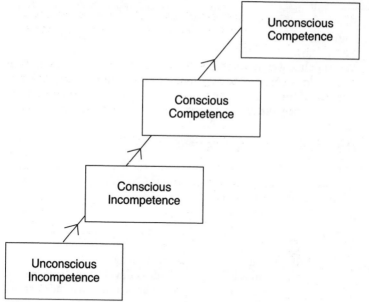

figure 8 four stages of learning from unconscious incompetence to unconscious competence

- **Unconscious Incompetence:** Imagine we had no idea what rapport was. We may have heard the word but didn't realize its importance in leading. Now you know why it's important but don't know how to do it. So we move to ...
- **Conscious Incompetence:** So we realize that we need to learn. We begin to read to be a better leader – and beyond. After practice we are now able to identify and use the three elements of rapport. People will have followed when you lead. Now we watch body posture, and listen to voice ... all at once. As we practise, and begin to notice the effects of rapport, we become skilled so we are now at:
- **Conscious Competence:** You know what to do and you still need to think about it. And as all the patterns we have learned blend into a smooth unit of behaviour, your ability to build rapport moves into the unconscious where it is available as ...
- **Unconscious Competence:** You do it naturally and without even thinking about it. You now may focus on the other elements of your leadership efforts, knowing that you can access your unconscious and retrieve the ability to build rapport when needed.

We may need to go through this sequence for each of the techniques described in the book. You may find that at times your learning does not give you the outcome you need. At times we 'unlearn' our skills when our leadership attempts do not get the results we wish. Using the feedback we move from unconscious competence to conscious competence, and begin to relearn. Our relearning moves us back to unconscious incompetence with more choices.

How we learn – the 4Mat system

In this section we present a powerful and elegant model of how we learn, a model that you can use to maximize your own learning and that of others.

Bernice McCarthy developed the 4Mat model after she had explored many other learning style models (Kolb, Honey, Jung, Myers-Briggs and Bates) that you may have experienced before. We need to be taught in four ways in order to be comfortable and successful while being stretched to develop other learning. We all have different learning preferences and learn more easily at one or two of the stages below.

The four preferences are:

- **Why?** Are we learning this piece of information? What are the benefits? Why is this important?
- **What?** Is it? What is the theory, the understanding?
- **How?** Do we do it? The experience of trying it out.
- **What if?** That might arise. A reflection and generation of questions.

Exercise on 4Mat

1 When you do not learn well it may be that one piece of the 4mat pattern was missing. Reflect on something that you needed to learn recently. Recall what happened. Were any stages left out?

2 Plan a learning session for another using the 4 stages of Why?, What?, How? and What If?. It may be coaching or mentoring someone through a skill that they have to follow. In your plan you may wish to reflect on the instruction for rapport building that followed the format of why, what, how and what if. You will find it useful to begin with a one line 'mini-what' to give people a label or title for the session and give them some idea of the area for learning. An example of a 4mat learning cycle is:

- Mini-what is 'now we would like to explore the topic of rapport building'
- Why is having rapport important to you?
- What? – detail of the components of rapport
- How? – a demonstration of rapport building and a chance to practise it in pairs
- What if? – a question-and-answer session.

3 Observe the increased effectiveness of the learning when using the format system to explain something.

Learning for leadership success

You have learned the building blocks for your Leadership. We have given you the belief that the skills you have learned will work. After all, if one can anyone can, and as you know, the leader with the most flexibility will succeed, and that you are in charge of your own behaviours. You can now use:

- The three-minute seminar of outcomes, observation and flexibility
- Your heightened awareness skills to notice voice, body and words
- Your ability to calibrate others' signals and build rapport using match–pace–lead
- Your understanding to learn more and to know better how to learn

Reflection

Many of our 'reflections' are short. However, such was Robert's success that this 'reflection' is longer than usual. Robert attended a three-day training programme in leadership skills that included rapport building. He was the Managing Director of a company that imported goods from the Far East and was due to leave for a major purchasing trip two weeks after the course. A major concern was that he always had to pay a considerable sum up front for the mouldings necessary for his products. During the course he had completed a set of well-formed outcomes that included building a relationship with a supplier of mouldings. He was prompted by one of the other participants to be sure to use the skills he had learned on the course when in negotiation with suppliers. This is his faxed reply to the other participants on the course:

'First of all the big news – I can confirm to you hand on heart – the leadership skills worked! No doubt before leaving I set out my targets for the trip – the clear goals identifying the best possible outcomes I could hope for on the trip. I was going to meet a manufacturer I had been trying to persuade to supply me for four years. Not only did I meet every one of those objectives in the first three days, I also saved a further USD $80,000 which I had been prepared to pay up front for the parts moulds for the new product. This is the first time ever in my experience that my business did not have to pay these upfront charges – yet before I got there I would have considered this impossible, and certainly did not include it as a target outcome. I used rapport, matching, pacing and leading as we were taught, and paid particular attention to my listening skills to monitor the reactions I was getting. I felt things were going so well I dared to make more demands of the manufacturer than I would ever have contemplated in the past, and everything worked! It was so easy I floated on clouds in brilliant blue skies all weekend. (Came down to earth when I got back to sunny UK this morning though!) Do please tell the others who attended the course what I managed for myself – it may help to actually provoke action. I know your fax to me telling me I **must** do NLP [neurolinguistic programming] on the trip was what prompted me to actually do the thing. Thank you for that – it really was what I needed. Now I won't be held back in the future – I am a believer.'

05

believe in: your cause, yourself, it being possible

In this chapter you will:
- explore the impact of beliefs on leadership
- deal with limiting beliefs
- recognize different levels of influence
- manage your state of mind and your state of being
- integrate any conflicting 'parts' of you that stop you leading
- be able to switch an undesirable reaction to a more desirable action

'The most effective leaders are those who first learn to lead themselves.'

Jim Kouzes and Barry Posner, *The Leadership Challenge*

Introduction

Having considered your style as a leader and explored the key building blocks of leadership, we will now look at what will help bring you and your actions as a leader into alignment, so that **you** get a sense of 'being sorted' and feel in a position to lead well.

In this chapter you will have the opportunity to deal with some of the elements about yourself and your surroundings that you know are not yet quite how you want them to be. A bit of personal fine-tuning for improved performance will work wonders!

While there is much that can take you forward in your development and transformation into the kind of leader you want to be, there may also be factors that can hold you back, factors that limit you. In this chapter, you will look at any limiting factors that might exist and explore ways of 'wiping them away'.

Beliefs

'They can because they think they can.'

Virail

This section is about enabling beliefs: *your* beliefs that allow you to do things. And they are the ideas, which for you are true. Beliefs are your operating principles for how you act. Some beliefs are about the physical world or the laws of nature – we don't walk off the tops of buildings or test each day that fire burns. However, we also have beliefs about people that are often less certain – that Joe is a 'lazy good for nothing' or 'a good worker'. When you believe something you act as if it is true, thus it becomes a difficult filter to shift.

There are many experiments that demonstrate the effects of beliefs on people. In Israel, army conscripts were divided into two groups with equal capabilities for gunnery training. One group was told they were specially selected as excellent learners. The other group was told nothing. Both groups received identical training. There was a very large difference in final performance between the two groups.

Similar experiments with the same differences in results have been completed in schools. For example, one group was told they had a high IQ and they were expected to do better than another group. And they did perform much better. The only difference between the two groups was the trainees' belief that they were in some way more capable than the other group. This type of self-fulfilling prophecy is known as the Pygmalion Effect.

Enabling beliefs

'If you believe you can or believe you can't, you are probably right.'

Henry Ford

You may also know people who believe things that hold them back in the particular circumstances that they find themselves in. For example, you may well recognize the difference in what can be achieved between one person who says they are 'too old' to try something and someone of a similar age who holds the belief that you are *never* 'too old' to do something. You have explored some 'new' beliefs – such as 'if one can anyone can' in Chapter 4.

The actions that you take as a leader are influenced greatly by the beliefs that you hold. A belief is a generalization about yourself and/or the world. Your beliefs are what you take to be true at any moment and they guide you in perceiving and interpreting your reality. Beliefs may be strongly held and they may enable you to act, or not. Beliefs are not cast in stone, they are only something that you have put together in your mind and so, where they are not helpful to you, beliefs can be changed. Beliefs can be enabling: they can help achieve success in leadership – or they can be limiting: holding you back from the success that you can achieve.

Consider the following example of enabling belief that happened to one of the authors (Catherine).

'I recently found myself locked out of my car with the keys inside it. I believed that we had lost the spare key, and thus there was no point in even thinking about where it could be. I began to plan an AA rescue mission. I rang my 10-year-old son at his childminder's to let him know I would be late. He thought we did have a key. He persuaded the childminder to drive him 10 miles to our home to search for the keys. His belief that he would find it kept him looking. He did find the key and arrived triumphant with the childminder to liberate me!'

It was my son's belief that there was a key that drove him to continue to look. If we/you can influence our beliefs we can create that drive in ourselves, and in others.

In a recent coaching session, we were fascinated to hear from a leader in community development who stated that one of her underlying beliefs is 'you can – you just have to find the way'. She applies this when working with communities that others have written off in the belief that nothing will work. Because others hold this belief, the sort of thinking that can unearth a solution is never applied. However, this community leader holds the belief that every community can achieve significant things in the ways that are right for them. Consequently, she believes it is worth spending energy and time working with residents to find out what will work and then working with other agencies with influence to back their proposals.

Consider, too, the sports leader who believes that a match can be won, when others believe that it is lost. One will play to win (and may) while the other will play for the final whistle without striving for victory. You will often only find what you are looking for.

Powerful beliefs can take people to places that they otherwise would not go:

Michael Jordan, the basketballer, believed: *'I never looked at the consequences of missing a big shot ... when you think about the consequences, you always think of a negative result.'*

Nelson Mandela, when in prison said, *'If you want to make peace with your enemy, you have to work with your enemy. Then he becomes your partner.'*

And Ernest Shackleton said, *'You can do anything when you believe in it, that's why I need to go back.'*

Being Churchill

Consider the beliefs of Churchill, who in 1930, wrote: *'Don't be content with things as they are. The earth is yours and the fullness thereof. Enter upon your inheritance, accept your responsibilities. Raise the glorious flags again, advance then upon your new enemies ... Don't take no for an answer. Never submit to failure. Do not be fobbed off with mere personal success or acceptance. You will make all kinds of mistakes; but as long as you are generous and true and also fierce ...'*

Beliefs are the bedrock of a person's behaviour. Imagine that Churchill did not hold these beliefs, or he held other ones, what would have happened then? He may even have had a day when he did or did not hold a particular belief. We can all recall a time when we just didn't hold one of our normal beliefs and it will have really affected our behaviour on that day.

Imagine what it would be like if *you* said the things that Churchill had said. Imagine what would be different in your leadership right now if you chose to take on some of the beliefs that are in Churchill's statement. You would not take 'No' for an answer, but you would find a way to influence to get the 'Yes' answer you want; you would not accept failure, you would go for success.

You are able to presuppose that Churchill's belief was yours for a moment or longer as it suits you. As you read this you might like to 'act as if' you held the belief and experience the difference it would make to your actions. If you like the difference, you could wear it, like a jacket, for a little longer, until you may find it is integrated into all that you do and has a benefit to you and those around you in the long term. If at any time holding the belief that you have taken on from someone else no longer feels congruent, you can then decide to put it down.

Trying on a belief and presupposing it were true

Let us try on for size some more of Churchill's belief statements! In doing this you are just presupposing that these statements are true for the time that holding this presupposition or temporary belief is valuable to you.

> *Don't be content with things as they are.*

Here Churchill's language implies that there is choice; that there are other ways of doing things, and that if you do something differently, you can change the situation and get a different outcome. Hold this belief and consider the things that are around you and imagine what it would be like if these things were, in your eyes, different from how they are now. Imagine that you could begin to change them, to have them be more the way they would need to be to achieve your objective. Now that you imagine them being different, what would be the things that you have done to change them? What do you hear yourself saying differently and how does it feel to know that they have been improved? Who would you be telling about the improvements that have been made and what would their reaction be? What beneficial impact will this have on your future and how does that future look with the change in place? What benefits would others need to see to have their experience of the changes be a good one, and how can you enable them to understand this?

As you have gone through this experience in your imagination as if it were real, your brain will have stored its own impression of doing it; it will have a memory of that imagination. Both real and imagined memories can have the same influence on your behaviour. For example, if you make up a pleasurable tune in your head or remember a real one they can both make you feel happier.

Why not try on another one of Churchill's beliefs?

Never submit to failure.

Another presupposition that underpins how we believe leaders are effective is – *There is no failure only feedback.*

You are always collecting data and feedback from other people about how things could better meet their needs. If you treat someone's feedback as a gift of data about what you could do differently, you will have more choice about how you could do something next time.

The words *never submit* are also powerful on their own. Submitting implies someone else having power over you. It is undoubtedly preferable to retain power over yourself so that you are in charge of your actions and reactions. One of the most powerful shifts we have ever witnessed was of an emergent leader who felt that the actions of another person (her Director) in ignoring her contributions and blanking her out were causing her harm. She was exhausted from the worry of it and continually ran conversations in her own head rehearsing what this person might be thinking, and what she would really like to say to him. Her internal analysis was all consuming. She was tired out by it and colleagues were starting to ask questions about her performance that just fuelled her propensity to think about it even more. She saw her Director as having huge power over her even though he was not interacting with her at all. She felt ignored, diminished and isolated.

Her mentor then pointed out that, as there was no transference of physical force from her Director to her, she was responsible for her own feelings, interpretations and actions and the harm they were doing her. She had the power and could either continue to persecute herself, continue to ignore her real worth, and shrink and isolate herself even more. The negative forces at work were her own, against herself – she could continue to submit herself to this or she could be confident and strong in her own self-belief and self-worth. The choice really was entirely her own. Her reaction to this realization was life changing. Her mentor suggested that she turn off this internal reaction and get on with doing the things that she did so well. She learnt that when her Director did acknowledge her or comment on her performance, it was only data and that she could choose to

---

EXERCISE: Define your beliefs

What do you believe are the things that you can do? Write below your top five beliefs about you as a leader.

1 _____

_____

2 _____

_____

3 _____

_____

4 _____

_____

5 _____

_____

These beliefs are likely to underpin all sorts of things that you do and achievements that you have already made. They are the sorts of things that others might want to copy from you, the way of being who you are that you already have and that others admire.

absorb it or not and know that she was in charge of this choice and the consequences it held. She may not have had the supportive environment that she would have liked but, nevertheless, she had the power over her own actions and re-actions and that seemed the most powerful thing of all.

So, taking on the belief of *never submit to failure* combined with believing in your own worth is a powerful combination indeed. A statement about failure is a perception expressed by one person from their view of the world. To the recipient of this expression it is just data. They have their own choices about how to process that data. It was Churchill who also said '*Success is going from failure to failure without a loss of enthusiasm.*' It is your judgement that makes the difference to your outcome.

More of Churchill's beliefs to 'try on for size' are:

'*Time is short and as much as possible must be done.*'

'*Kites rise highest against the wind – not with it.*'

'*Applause for good work is worth having.*'

'*It is necessary to be flexible in one's plans, for the achievement of goals.*'

Limiting beliefs

'*The ideal is in thyself; the impediment, too, is in thyself.*'
Thomas Carlyle

The above examples show how a belief can be very enabling; however, a limiting belief can have the opposite effect and hold us back from doing something.

If you accept that a belief is something that you have constructed for yourself and that those beliefs that do not serve you well can be reconstructed to be more useful, then you have a powerful tool to increase your effectiveness as a leader.

Think about a belief that is true for you that you consider holds you back. Now think about someone you admire who does not hold this belief and is more able or resourceful because of this different belief. Imagine what it would be like if you held their beliefs. After the next example of this in action, you will do an exercise that demonstrates the power of this for yourself.

Case study: Pamela and Moira

An example of the power of holding different beliefs is evident where Pamela holds the belief that 'people are out to get her and put her down'. This limits Pamela in all sorts of circumstances. She feels unable to trust others and she is not willing to do anything until she thinks it is perfect. This results in her spending long periods of time behind her desk, mulling over all the pitfalls and guarding herself against anyone who may come into the room. Her guarded welcome to visitors is often matched by a guarded response. When people do give her feedback she is constantly looking for the negative intention in what they have said or imagining the significance of what they have not said. All in all, although Pamela's positive intention in holding this belief is to protect herself from harm or harsh criticism, it really does hold her back. Pamela creates her own reality.

Her colleague Moira, however, holds the belief that 'people really want to hear her ideas and they want her to do well'. Any feedback or criticism they give Moira is just to help her get better at what she is doing. Consequently, Moira is willing to express and share her ideas at an early stage, which allows her to refine her ideas and performance as she goes along. She has her door open, welcomes people who pop in and talks with enthusiasm about the ideas she is developing. There is a regular buzz of conversation coming from her office. Because Moira thinks feedback is valuable, she invariably thanks people for the comments they make which, in turn, makes them feel good about giving her comments. This sets up a virtuous circle of feedback and improvement. The people who have given feedback or criticism then feel involved in Moira's performance and applaud the improvements she makes and her end results. Moira, like Pamela, creates her own reality.

What would it be like if Pamela took on the beliefs of Moira for just one project. Pamela could, for the purposes of this exercise, presuppose that Moira's beliefs were her own and then act accordingly. She would be 'acting as if' she was Moira, and thinking through 'what would Moira do in this situation?': How would Moira approach this? How would Moira feel about expressing her ideas and getting comments back that will improve her performance? What words does Moira use to thank others for their comments and criticisms? Pamela can then act as if she was Moira and experience all the differences inside herself as she accepts comments as being valuable; feel good about herself as she shows flexibility in considering ideas which may then spark off more ideas of her own; and be confident in the belief that comments are given because others want her to do well and achieve her potential. Pamela, holding these beliefs, would act in an entirely different way with her own new virtuous circle of experience, which would be a very resourceful thing to do. After she has done this, she may realize she could take this choice wherever she chooses in the future.

'When you see a worthy person endeavour to emulate him. When you see an unworthy person then examine your inner self.'

Confucius

EXERCISE: To utilize powerful beliefs from others

You, like Pamela, can adopt other beliefs. This exercise allows you to try out a belief that is serving someone else well as a leader. When you have experienced the usefulness of the new belief then you can expand the exercise to include more, or exchange some of your beliefs that may be holding you back.

- Think of an admired other person.
- List the beliefs they hold that serve them well in the kind of situation you are thinking about.
- 'Act as if' you, too, held these beliefs for the period of the project you wish to do.
- Now that you can presuppose these beliefs to be true, what can you see yourself doing, hear yourself saying, and what feelings do you get as a result of these changes?
- Note how you are free to do things in a different way and the new choices that this gives you.
- Note what you are free from.

Doing this exercise allows you to give yourself more choice, and have access to more resources. You can then choose if you want to hold any of these beliefs for a longer period of time. You will notice that, to do this, you may now want to consider how this new belief fits in with other beliefs that you already hold. Beliefs are not static. You have the opportunity to fine-tune and realign your beliefs and how they impact on each other.

In this first part of the chapter you have looked at how enabling beliefs push people towards goals and how limiting beliefs hold them back. We have also explored Churchill's beliefs and, through the voices of Pamela and Moira, how powerful changing beliefs can be. You have tried out new beliefs and will have found that taking on enabling beliefs gives you choice and choice gives you flexibility and, as Alice finds out, you can practise changing your beliefs:

'I can't believe that!' said Alice.

'Can't you?' the Queen said in a pitying tone, 'try again. Draw a long breath, and shut your eyes.'

Alice laughed, 'There is no use trying' she said, 'One can't believe impossible things.'

'I dare say you haven't had much practice,' said the Queen. 'When I was your age I always did it for half an hour a day. Why, sometimes I believed as many as six impossible things before breakfast.'

Lewis Carroll, *Alice Through The Looking Glass*

Levels of influence

One truth stands firm. All that happens in world history rests on something spiritual. If the spiritual is strong, it creates world history. If it is weak it suffers world history.

Albert Schweitzer

There are different levels of change and influence. It is apparent that some changes, which are well intentioned and even generous, do not always change what really happens. They may be operating at the wrong level.

Someone like James, in this description, may already be familiar to you. James was determined to make a change in how his career was going. He didn't see himself as a high flyer but he definitely thought he might be able to improve his chances by doing something positive. He changed his office around, went to a colour consultant and bought new clothes, he bought a computer and had classes in IT and word processing, and even bought some 'high impact' motivational tapes – and yet still there was no substantial change either in James or in what happened to him and he was heard to say 'I knew it wouldn't work for me'.

In the case of James he had made changes to his environment (changing his office and buying a new computer), he had changed some behaviours (dressed differently) and even improved his skills and capabilities (learned to word process and use the computer), but the change in his life and how he felt about himself did not alter, because he had not attended to the more powerful influences of beliefs – about himself ('I knew it wouldn't work'), his identity ('I am not a high flyer') and purpose (what is the higher reason for doing things?).

Yours and everyone's world is made up of many different influences or levels. Leadership involves co-ordinated changes of yourself and others across different levels at different times to create of the world that you as a leader envisage. These levels can be shown as in Figure 9, to illustrate a hierarchy of influence.

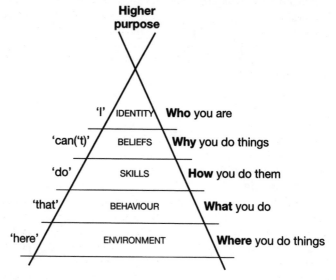

figure 9 hierarchy of influence

In working through the technique set out in Figure 9, you will be invited to consider what drives you on and what holds you back. You can then choose to make changes that will improve your effectiveness and sense of alignment as a leader: it is a rewarding experience that can have some real benefits for you and for others.

At the very top of this model is the level of *mission* that represents the **wider purpose** in your life. For some, this is some sort of spirituality or wider reason for life. It is at this level that mission and vision statements are expressed.

Then there is the level that represents **who** you are. The *identity* level. The 'I am' statements or even the 'I am not' statements. I am a fighter or I am a pacifist. Your role and sense of self are held at this level.

Any process is influenced by the *beliefs and values* that people hold. You have explored beliefs earlier in this chapter. Beliefs about what is so and not so, about what is right and not right, about what can be and what can't. It is the **why** of leadership. These beliefs are often imprinted early in your life and they do not have to remain unchanged forever! Sometimes they will serve you well and at other times they will hold you back. Overarching beliefs are a set of values that guide you through life and the way you live it. They become powerful motivating guidelines for what you do and help you to stay on a stable track. An example of a value might be 'all life is precious', or 'honesty is imperative', or 'family life (in whatever form) is the centre of stability'.

People have refined *skills and capabilities* that are well-honed clusters of behaviours that fit together to allow them to do things in a way that is effective and almost effortless and second nature. You may see yourself as a competent communicator, or as a good thinker. There are well-worn patterns that relate to inner structures and cognitive capabilities. They are the **how** of how things are done.

The individual actions that people take is described as the *behaviour level*. Different people behave in different ways and take actions that will not be the same as yours. **What** people do is fascinating. The capabilities of the communicator can be broken down into behaviours – e.g. listening, chatting, speech, use of language etc. The thinker would have for example the skills of analysis and synthesis. What makes up these different skills? Your behaviours and actions enable you to demonstrate what you actually do. What are the behaviours and actions that you take that are effective or ineffective? How do these look from the eyes of others? If you know what you or others do at this level then you can choose to do things differently if that would serve you better. Another example of choice.

Finally look for the **where and when,** the environment and the physical places. This environment also indicates the **who else** is involved – e.g. your competition, the market, your customers or your community. This level also includes equipment, materials, systems, reports and paperwork.

So, starting at the base of the model, what is it at this level that you need to change or pay attention to? Are you operating in the right environment? Have you created the right environmental conditions in the light of all that is in the levels above it? For instance, if you hold a belief that all staff have a valuable part to play in your enterprise, does this reflect itself in the environment you provide for them to work in?

There is a natural hierarchy in these levels. Each level above is more abstract and more powerful than those below and has a greater degree of impact on those below. A change at an upper level will cascade and permeate through those below it. A change at a lower level may influence those above and it may not. Lower level changes are definitely not as powerful as higher level changes.

You can run a limiting belief through this model using the statement:

'I'	(identity)
'Can ('t)'	(belief)
'Do'	(skill and capability)
'That'	(behaviour)
'Here'	(environment)

Listen for where the emphasis lies in the statement, and this may provide a powerful indicator as to which level the change needs to be made. Let's take the statement 'I can't dance the tango at a wedding'. Play with the emphasis at different levels. If you emphasis the 'I' you hold the limitation at an identity level. You cannot ever imagine that you could do the tango as you are not a dancer. If you emphasize the word '**wedding**' then the limiting factor is more likely to be the environment and changing the location may resolve the matter. You can dance the tango at the dance hall but not in front of relatives at a wedding. Many times we make an intervention at a level that does not match the person limitation and thus we are unlikely to manage the change that is needed.

Good leaders ensure attention is paid to every level in this model. To bring about the world that you want others to subscribe to, you need alignment through all the levels. The most powerful impact will be felt by things being right at the top, but that is no excuse to neglect the bottom.

So, to follow up the example of James, he had made changes at the lower end levels of environment, behaviour and a little at skill and capability level. However, he has clearly not addressed how he holds his own identity and beliefs. When he changes these, for example, from 'I am not a high flyer' to something like 'I am an emergent leader', everything below can begin to change and realign to support this identity.

Here is an exercise to run through for yourself to see where your leadership could benefit from some finer alignment and tuning.

EXERCISE

What is your vision or mission and what is the relationship to the wider purpose or system that you operate within?

My mission as a leader is to _____

_____

What is your identity or role in relation to this vision and mission?

I am a leader because I am _____

_____

What key beliefs and values are encapsulated in your vision and mission?

The values that are important in my leadership are _____

_____

The beliefs that support me in leading others are

_____

What capabilities and skills will you use to accomplish your vision and mission and what behaviours will be indicators that you are doing this?

My capabilities as a leader are _____

_____

What particular behaviours will be evident when all this is in tune and working well?

The behaviours that are evident and support my leadership are

_____

What context and environment will you do this in?

I am a leader in the context of_____

_____

These are the things I will get right in my environment _____

_____

For many people reading this statement from top to bottom will give a clear picture of the path that they intend to follow.

As you read yours, you will be aware of anything that does not ring true and be able to revisit and adjust your statement until it hits just the right note.

A visual representation of this can be a powerful metaphor to help people get an even clearer picture. You may already have an image that crystallizes all the above for you, or you may wish to find or create one. It can be a powerful anchor for the whole experience you are going to create.

EXAMPLE: Serge Kahili King

We recently had the joy of meeting Serge Kahili King, a leader from Hawaii. It was great to talk to someone who is a good example of having his life aligned at every level. And most powerful of all was the identity he holds for himself as a shaman and the beliefs that underpin this identity.

Dr Serge Kahili King has created an effective organization, Aloha International, which promotes the teaching of the Hawaiian Healing tradition throughout the world. The tradition has many 'urban' uses; maintaining a career, improving relationships, influencing others and creating the vision. The promotion of the tradition is through a worldwide network of shaman healers who utilize courses, seminars, museums, and local groups. Dr King started the organization in 1973, dismantled it when he thought it was not achieving its purpose, and recreated the organization in the 1990s. A key aspect of the tradition is belief in the power of mind – that the world is what we think it is, and that there are no limits (except those we set ourselves). The belief is that we can achieve what we want if we focus on it. Dr King's views are:

'I have clear beliefs about how to get the best from my associates. When I first started the organization, it didn't work. People began to interpose themselves between the members and me. I took the organization down to zero – and now there is no hierarchy – I don't see myself at the top. I see myself at the centre, keeping communication lines going, and facilitating the organization. Now there are no barriers between me and any part of the organization.

'We keep the members centred on the focus through frequent meetings and consultations – and the social aspects are important. Our commitment to the aims of the organization is formally repeated annually – the commitment is not only to the spirit of Huna but also to a commitment to work together.

'As we are a rapidly developing organization, there is always a need for change – and my organization is a very specialized one. All have their own careers. They are not people who by nature take easily to being told what to do. The upside of this nature is that their feedback on a change is valuable and if they do take something on you really get success. The downside is that you have to be very creative in introducing change. I don't present something as an option unless I have experienced it. Then I inform them and offer it for them to do. I never say this is what we must do, this is the way we will work.

'I know I have been successful when some people have forgotten when I introduced the change.'

Manage your state – manage your outcome

'Leadership is more a state than an activity.'

Gilles Pajou

Lucy was a successful manager of a Leisure Centre. She was able to manage a complex business that operates 360 days a year, seven days a week and 18 hours a day. Lucy had respect from staff, customers and the elected Councillors who oversee the services. The other thing that Lucy had was 'up days' and 'down days'. On one occasion she had to make a presentation to representatives from all the clubs and societies that used the busy sports centre in Central London. She had been asked to convince them of a new programming balance that was being introduced to allow more access to services for the general public. Before the meeting Lucy was operating out of 'down day' mode. What was printable of her language included 'They will never believe me', 'I hate doing presentations' and 'I shouldn't be making this presentation – can't someone else do it?' Her posture was slumped, her energy low, her pace of voice slow and generally not oozing confidence. We can all imagine how her address went down.

You have read that leadership is not a formula. Moreover you work in an unpredictable world so cannot plan what to do in detail in advance. You may have the ability to predict some aspects of the future, and not all of them, so you will be wasting your time and energy as a leader if all you do is have a detailed plan of exactly how you are going to do all the things necessary to achieve your well-formed outcomes. Preparation and knowledge are important but to just *be* all that you can be is paramount and the *doing* will then be more likely to take care of itself. Leaders are helped by having inner alignment at all levels and then further helped by using all the intuition and sensory awareness to adjust what they do to fit in perfectly with the situations that arise.

Wouldn't it be fantastic to have a process that enables you and Lucy to turn a down day into an up day and be in the best possible state to deal with any situation that you have to face? Sportsmen are very good at achieving this state of being to aid peak performance and as leaders we can learn a great deal from them.

Have you ever noticed that tendency for yourself when you have a great day, when everything works well, is 'on song' and feels fantastic? Dennis Lillee, the great Australian cricketer and fast bowler, used to show that he had days when everything clicked and worked brilliantly. For him it was only a very occasional experience to 'get out of the wrong side of the bed' and sense that things would not produce the results that he and others expected of him. He knew he was highly capable as a fast bowler, and even so he also knew that he had to get himself into the right state of mind and body to produce high performance cricket by the start of play. Sometimes this was a matter of physical well-being but more often it was a matter of mental state and self-belief, or lack of it, that made the difference.

No sporting icon can afford the luxury of too many 'down' days and the sporting public would certainly not be tolerant of that.

Clearly any misalignment in relation to the levels that we have considered earlier in this chapter will prevent some from attaining peak performance. And so there is also a role for the alignment of physiology and the internal state of being that you know you experience when there is 'just no stopping you'.

So, how do we attain that state for peak performance? As in the example of Dennis Lillee, you need the capability from talent and practice. Nevertheless up days and down days still exist. How can we have many more up days, and in particular be able to produce the performances that will make all the difference when it really matters? One answer is 'anchoring', and we now discuss this.

Anchoring

Let's look at how this might have been for Dennis Lillee in his performance on the cricket pitch. (This could also be true for almost any sportsperson stepping into any big arena.) Lillee may have instinctively used a process called anchoring. Sportsmen use it all the time, for example US Open tennis 2004 finalist Lleyton Hewitt said *'every time I step onto the Wimbledon Court, I take my positive memories with me.'*

Anchoring is when an external stimulus triggers an internal emotional state. The trigger can be through any one of the senses. The sound of a song (external stimulus) takes you straight back to feelings (internal emotional state) you had about someone or somewhere the first time you heard it. The sound of the crowd triggers the memory and feeling of winning the last match. Perhaps you can relate to the smell of disinfectant (external stimulus) that can create the same nervousness you had when last at the dentist or hospital. A visual anchor might be a photograph or a picture, a view of someone's face or even a colour that has significance. Seeing an image, such as a house where you used to live, can unlock strong associated feelings with being there. A taste, such as that of jelly, may take you straight back to perhaps a childhood experience.

Positive and negative anchors can be set up. Positive ones can create 'up' days and negative ones 'down' days. The most extreme negative anchors are phobias where we have an irrational disproportionate response to an event, real or even imagined. We look at dealing with phobias in Chapter 11.

Creating great feelings

How could you create positive states for your leadership equivalent of a big sporting arena? Perhaps you want to feel confident just before making a presentation. The following exercise shows how you connect a positive internal feeling to a unique but replicable external stimulus (a gesture, sound or anchor) that you can use any time you want the feeling of confidence.

EXERCISE: An anchor for confidence

1 Choose a state that you want to have at your disposal, something you really want. We will use confidence as an example.

2 Choose an anchor or gesture that is unique and that you can easily and discretely replicate. An example would be squeezing your wrist.

3 Recall a time when you had confidence. Just the right sort of confidence that you need for your presentation. It could be from anywhere in your life's experience. Re-experience fully that sensation of confidence and as you do and it begins to feel really good create your anchor by squeezing your wrist.

4 Hold the pressure on your squeezed wrist for a few seconds and release the pressure just before the good feeling of being confident begins to subside.

5 Think about something else for a minute (like what you had for breakfast). This helps break your state and clear your mind ready for the next step.

6 Test your anchor by making the gesture (squeezing your wrist) and re-experiencing the positive feeling of confidence that now comes with it. You have just set off your anchor!

7 Now re-print this link between internal emotional feeling (confidence) with this external stimulus (squeezing your wrist) by repeating steps 2 to 5. Do this at least five times to make the link really strong.

8 Now, think about the next time you need to feel confident. As you imagine this scenario set off your anchor (squeeze your wrist) and now have the feeling of being in that future situation *with* your confidence. Notice how much better it feels.

You now have a process for anchoring. It is valuable to you and it is a valuable coaching tool for you to help get peak performance from others. Often people will know that they need more than just one internal resource or feeling to perform really well. Let us look at what Lillee might have needed and at the same time explore a technique for stacking several needed feelings onto one anchor.

Anchoring more than one state – stacking anchors

What would be the 'tailor-made state' that Dennis Lillee would need to create for himself to perform at his peak in an all-important Test Match? What would be the inner resources that he needs to anchor for himself so that when he walks out onto the cricket ground he is in exactly the right frame of mind?

Perhaps the inner resources needed would have been:

- Confidence in his team mates
- Knowledge of his own ability
- Experience of performing against the odds
- Ability to motivate his team mates

Imagine how Lillee could begin this process by remembering a time when he had complete confidence in his team mates. He had an almost symbiotic existence with wicket keeper Rod Marsh that allowed them to take an extraordinary number of 343 catches behind the wicket in the combination of 'bowled Lillee caught Marsh'. In particular he could recall the Greg Chappell wicket in an interstate game when this synthesis was at its most powerful. In this instance Marsh and Lillee had worked out a strategy to dismiss Chappell who was in great form. They set a field that tempted Chappell to go for a hook shot (which is one of the most elegant shots in Chappell's range) to a Lillee high pitching bouncer (that arrives at about head height). When Chappell was ready to face the incoming ball Marsh was behind the stumps in his normal position, he touched the top of his head, a movement which most spectators took as a signal to Lillee to bowl a bouncer. As Lillee reached his delivery stride, Marsh took off and began running towards the outfield fine leg position where, as Chappell gloriously hooked Lillee, Marsh was waiting and took the catch! Chappell was out and furious at his dismissal. Lillee experienced confidence in his team mates indeed.

As Lillee recalls the image of Marsh signalling him and the great feelings that went with that memory, he could anchor it by squeezing the cricket ball. Now if he was to squeeze the cricket ball, he could re-access that whole experience and all the jubilant feelings about working with Marsh that he had.

And yet he needs more resources for his state to be just right. He needs knowledge of his own ability. To 'get' this he could recall a time when he had real confidence in his own knowledge and ability. It might have been recalling his ability to reconstruct his back after serious injury and adjust his delivery stride through painstaking analysis of his movements that resulted in him returning to Test cricket in better shape than ever. Perhaps the essence of this moment was when he returned to playing. As he recalls himself walking back to the players' pavilion and hearing the affectionate and appreciative applause of the crowd and his own internal voice saying 'you've done it' he could stack this anchor on top of the one for confidence in his team mates by squeezing the ball.

With two states anchored let us move on to the next one – 'performing against the odds'. At the Centenary Test in Melbourne in 1977, Australia were not favoured to win. And Lillee had been in this situation as a cricketer before. There had been times when matches had seemed out of grasp, when they were heading for loss then against the odds they had succeeded. Lillee might recall vividly such an occasion and in particular hear himself saying that every ball can take a wicket and then anchor this sensation on the ball as he had the others.

Finally he needs to recall the state that represents his ability to motivate others. He could focus on another match and the way he talked to his colleagues and met their gaze so that the unspoken message of 'we can do this' was passed between them. Lillee could anchor the feeling that he had when others responded to his gaze and he knew that they were on the same wavelength as him. He knew he had convinced them to do it. Just at the moment when he recalled the look that went from him to them he could anchor that feeling by squeezing the ball.

Now he has all four required states stacked through one anchor of squeezing the ball. All he has to do to get exactly in the right frame of mind, state of being, and level of energy is to squeeze the ball and re-associate with all the feelings that will mean he steps onto the ground with a power and aura around him that can turn a match.

Lessons for Lucy

One of the major factors that has allowed Lucy to move on in her career has been her ability to manage her state and to get herself into the frame of mind and body that she needs to convince others (and herself) to follow the strategic social plans that she now implements. Her career may never have progressed beyond the leisure centre without this skill in state management.

EXERCISE for a tailor-made state

1 Think of a situation in which you need to perform well as a leader.

2 List the internal resources (four or five of them) that you will need to achieve at least the result you dream of. (They might be courage, self-belief, insight, attentiveness, tenacity, trust.) Number them 1 to 5.

3 Now recall a time when you had 1. Just the right sort of 1 that you will need in the future situation. Associate with it and recall what you see, what you hear both outside and inside yourself, and how you feel when this is just the right sort of 1. Just as you are experiencing this sensation and just before the feeling peaks, anchor the experience by a unique trigger or anchor. You may consider pressing your thumb into your thigh, something that is unique but replicable.

4 Now, break your state by taking a deep breath and stepping back for a moment. Think of something else for a moment, like what you had yesterday for breakfast.

5 Now you are ready to anchor state number 2. Recall a time when you had exactly the right sort of 2. It can be from anywhere in your life's experience. Associate with that experience by recalling what you see, hear and feel. Notice anything that is particularly strong about this experience, and focus on that. Just as you feel this sensation reaching a peak, fire the anchor – if you chose pressing your thigh then do that to anchor the state.

6 Break your state again.

7 Repeat the stacking of the experiences up to number 5 if you have that many by adding them on to the same anchor and breaking the state each time.

8 Now let us see if you have achieved a tailor-made resourceful state for the occasion that you are thinking of. You can test how well you have this resourceful state at your immediate disposal. Imagine the scenario you first thought of at the beginning of this exercise. Now just before this scenario commences, fire your anchor (press your thumb onto your thigh if you chose that anchor) and re-experience all the good sensations that come with it. Now imagine with all those resources in play, in sight, and on form how you are responding really well to the imagined situation because you know that you can do this and that you have all the resources and flexibility that are needed to achieve what you want, and beyond.

Getting others ready for peak performance

As a leader you can also coach others through this process to help them be in the resourceful state that would be needed for peak performance. Your ability to lead is greatly enhanced by techniques that you can apply to others to get them in a state to perform at their peak. What a gift to be able to give someone.

Dealing with internal conflict

'A leader who doesn't hesitate before he sends his nation into battle is not fit to be a leader.'

Golda Meir

Lucy in the previous section has now been able to generate a resourceful state and yet at a deeper level she still wasn't performing the way she wanted to. She told us 'a part of me wants to take risks and a part of me doesn't'. Her statement allows us to see that there can almost be a competition going on within ourselves, and that when this sense of competing intentions and motivations exists within ourselves it can lead to a sense of tension within oneself.

In any situation that you face, you also face the possibility of having an internal dilemma about what will be the best course of action to take. When you consider this dilemma you may notice that one part of you tells you that you should go ahead and take the action that you are thinking of, whilst another part is cautioning care and asking you to hold back. There may even be another part or voice that starts to nag you about your inability to make a decision. The way that they keep talking at cross-purposes inside your head may be quite agitating to you and may be a drain on your energies.

The internal world that you have will be familiar to you, and probably quite strange to others. We have known some successful leaders talking to us in coaching sessions about the parts that they have. Sometimes there are two or three that are clearly evident to them, and we have worked with one successful international marketing executive who definitely had seven parts!

So let us look at what these are all about and work through a process that can help you come to decisions that feel spot on and allow you to skip the agitating and time-wasting processes that may currently be restraining you.

A Director recently said 'it would be easier to get actual people together in a room to come to an agreement than it would be to get parts of myself to agree on what I am going to do'. The reality is that accommodating your parts so that they agree a course of action such that they are all satisfied is not as difficult as it might seem, and it is very similar in principle to different people coming to an agreement.

The exercise below may, at first reading, seem a little unusual to some people, and not to others. So we would like you to suspend judgement for a moment and work your way to the end of the exercise where you will realize just how helpful this may be.

A presupposition of leadership is that *Every behaviour has a positive intention*. For instance, at a personal level smoking has, for the individual who smokes, a positive intention – e.g. nicotine high, sociability, something to do with their hands – even though at another level people know it is bad for them. In a work environment the individual who, for example, talks over others, has a positive intention for himself or herself. He may have the intention of expressing his ideas powerfully. The process described below uses the principle of separating the behaviour from the intention and generating alternative behaviours that are more acceptable and still fulfil the intention. This generation of alternative behaviours gives the individual more choice. Choice gives more flexibility and the person with the most flexibility has most influence over any system.

EXERCISE: Resolving internal conflict

This process will allow you to generate more choices in your behaviours. The six-step process uses the principle of separating the behaviour from the intention.

Imagine for this example a part of you objects to a proposal and another part of you wants to do it. You have an internal conflict or dilemma about what to do. You may want to imagine these two parts in your hands – one in the left hand and one in the right hand.

Step 1. Ask the part that objects to the proposal, what positive intention it has in making the objection. Just listen and then acknowledge that this intention to you as a person is a valuable one even if the way it is being expressed at the moment is not that helpful. You may want to give this part a label or a name for ease of reference. Let's call it Part A 'objector'.

Step 2. Ask the other part (Part B; let's call it 'driver') that is proposing the action what positive intention it has to you. Acknowledge and thank Part B for this intention – this will let you know the underlying motivation of Part B in doing what it is doing.

Step 3. Ask Part B 'driver' to suggest other ways of achieving the outcome that it wants that takes account of what might satisfy Part A's 'objector' positive intentions. Think of at least three new choices, and say them out loud. (If you can't think of three ask your creative part to make some suggestions.)

Step 4. Ask Part A 'objector' if it is satisfied by any of these alternative proposals and if it would be willing to go along with one of them for an agreed period of time, remembering that Part B 'driver' has a positive intention in wanting to take this action. Keep the discussion going between the parts until they can agree.

Step 5. Now that these two parts have agreed an action, ask if there are any other parts that are not happy with the proposal. If there is, create and name Part C and go through steps 2, 3, and 4, until it too is happy to agree to the proposal.

Step 6. Now imagine yourself taking the new agreed step and experience in advance how it will feel and hear all the parts supporting it. You may want to bring your hands together at this point to represent a new integrated strategy for action. You will now feel very motivated to take this action and make it successful.

Changing habitual reactions fast!

Winning is a habit. Unfortunately so is losing.

Vince Lombardi

Stimulus begets response

'Every time it happens I react in the same way that gets me into trouble!' said Helen who was a talented human resource manager who had a quick and wicked wit that landed her in difficult situations more than once. On this occasion she had made a cutting and sarcastic remark (that got a great laugh by the way) about a member of the Executive team (Steve) who was absent at the time. Steve was a rich source of material for Helen as he was an innovative (some would say 'whacky') thinker. Helen's comment on this occasion was 'Which part of *no* does the intergalactic traveller not understand today?' Everyone laughed and yet it left an uneasy feeling in people as they left the room. 'What else might she say when they were absent – and who would laugh then?', they may have mused.

It is useful to address a response to a situation that you experience that causes you to act in a predictable but unhelpful way. We all run these patterns, and sometimes we have them ingrained as much in our home-life as we do in our working situation. You know the ones – you come home and someone's question or tone of voice just seems to make you respond with an unhelpful comment or an unattractive voice tone all of your own. A sort of stimulus/response with no gap for thought occurs. Something just triggers you off and almost without helping yourself, you hear yourself making your standard type of response. Well you can change these reactions using a simple technique that enables leaders to choose a more helpful way of responding.

Changing your reaction in a 'swish'

Thinking of how such a technique is helpful to leaders we might consider how Churchill may have been able to use this approach. His antipathy to Mr Gladstone was well known. Churchill had a wicked wit as evidenced by this quote '*Mr. Gladstone read Homer for fun, which I thought served him right.*' If, however, Churchill had allowed this type of reaction to automatically kick in, as may have been his instinctive reaction, it would not have served him well in many situations. His automatic reaction may have been to respond to a Gladstone comment as if he wanted to put him down. A reaction that allowed him to avoid this automatic route and instead to re-program his first reaction to be something more helpful may have resembled this process.

A technique has been developed called 'swish' which allows us to choose the response behaviour we want to a particular stimulus, instead of being trapped into the response we have habitually given. Whether it is Churchill, the HR Director, Helen or yourself, leadership can benefit from the technique of Swish.

In the analysis of Helen, she has a link between the image she creates in her head of Executive team member Steve, and the compulsion to make a joke. Every time she thought of his face, she heard herself making a sarcastic remark. In the work we did with Helen, we asked her to describe the moment when getting an image of Steve she begins to formulate her comments. We asked her to fully re-experience making these remarks including the moment seconds later when she would cringe at what she had said. We asked her to make this image of her reacting to Steve, big and bright, close, in focus. Now we asked her to make an image of her self being a more resourceful type of person reacting in a more appropriate way. The image of herself that she would be proud of in response to the stimulus of seeing his face in her mind or in reality in a meeting. We encouraged Helen to identify the behaviour in response to thinking of Steve that she thought would be more resourceful and helpful to her. Her response was to show people she was interested in them and to show genuine curiosity about what her unmet needs were. We asked her to make this image smaller, darker, and to put this image in the far corner of the first picture. At this point Helen was adamant that she did not want to look at the big bright picture as she was much more attracted to the smaller darker image.

Because Helen's mind is now committed to this image that is small, dark and in one corner, she may literally want to 'swish' the new behaviour image until it obliterates the old bright image and becomes the new picture she wants to see. It can be programmed in as her new regular pattern by repeating the swish technique five or six times. Between each swish, make sure you clear all images in front of you so you are ready to 'Swish' again. Never swish in both directions or you literally will not know if you are coming or going (see Figure 10 on page 94).

EXERCISE: New behaviour trigger

You can now bring to mind a pattern that you know you run that is habitual in response to a certain trigger or situation. Here are the steps you can follow:

1 Identify the unwanted behaviour or reaction that you wish to change and what triggers that behaviour or reaction.

2 Create a bright, associated, large image of the trigger behaviour. It may be an internal feeling that you can fully associate with or it may be an external image that you fully re-experience the memory. Really enrich this image with all the sub-detail that is there.

3 Now put that image aside and clear your mind. Perhaps think of something entirely different for a moment.

4 Construct the preferred behaviour, what you would really like to be like when the trigger occurs. Keep this image disassociated. This means you are looking at it rather than 'living' it. Give this new image all the resources that you need to have in that situation. It will be an image of you being the sort of you that you really want to be. Make it compelling and realistic, and notice how this will fit with the rest of your life. Make sure this image remains disassociated at this point. Make this image smaller and darker until it is tiny.

5 Put this image aside and clear your mind.

6 Bring back the big, bright associated image of the unwanted behaviour and put a frame around it. Place in one corner the small darker disassociated image of the desired behaviour.

7 Now swish the small, darker, disassociated image up and over the other image so that it completely floods your view with the image of the new desired behaviour and now associate with this new behaviour. Live it and enjoy it. Separate out the images again and repeat this step 7 up to five times until it happens automatically and becomes your new automatic reaction.

This technique is a powerful and fast way to change a behaviour pattern that you currently have that limits you in your abilities to be an even more effective leader.

figure 10 how to 'swish'

Learning for leadership success

You have:

- Understood the impact and power of holding enabling beliefs
- Worked through a series of levels for leadership excellence and tested your own leadership approaches using this technique
- Recognized how to anchor a resourceful state of mind and being
- Discovered a process for getting all parts of you to agree a way of proceeding in any situation
- Learnt the fast behaviour change process known as Swish

Reflections

Aloha John and Catherine,

You recently asked about my beliefs as a leader. The most important thing is my focus. The clarity of my focus helps the clarity of the focus of those who are working for me. If I lose my focus they lose theirs. I create the focus by knowing what I'm doing. Even before I created the organisation I wrote the focus down and never changed it. It's now so habitual it's in the back of my mind and it wouldn't be correct to say I don't lose sight of it. I'm holding it out in front of me. It's the foundation of what I do. So that's how I build the focus. The focus is the purpose of the organization.

Dr Serge Kahili King

Aloha International

'Teaching and practising the seven principles of Huna and to spread the Aloha spirit.'

06

unlocking patterns of communication

In this chapter you will learn:

- how your message may be *deleted*, *generalized* and *distorted* through understanding the leadership communication model
- how to communicate especially using the *senses*
- that your *wisdom as a leader* flows from seeing things from three different perspectives

> 'The first task of a leader is to define reality.'
>
> Max Defree, former chairman of the
> Hermann Miller company.

Introduction

In Chapter 3, you saw the importance of knowing what you really want and creating your own 'well-formed outcome'. As a leader, creating that well-formed outcome provides the spur to action for the follower. In creating that outcome, you are creating a *future reality* for your followers, for individuals to know what to strive for. This chapter concerns how individuals create a reality for themselves; if you know how an individual creates their reality you can then begin to help them to create a *reality* that is in line with your leadership outcomes.

Case study: 'why can't they understand?'

Claudia, the CEO of an organization in the hospitality sector, had decided on a new mission statement. She decided on the phrase 'Ladies and gentlemen serving ladies and gentlemen' – adapted from the Ritz Carlton Group. She feels quite pleased about that phrase. She presented the statement of her mission as a challenge to her key staff to change the way they work. Her delivery was a well-crafted PowerPoint presentation, which she had worked on until 4.00am the previous morning. During the presentation she was concerned that the reaction she was getting was poor. Many of the staff seemed disinterested and unexcited. Indeed, the response to the presentation was disappointing. The negative comments were in the majority, with only one positive comment:

- 'Change makes me feel down. I'm never sure what is happening around here.'
- 'It's typical – a new statement of intent – and there won't be the training and communication to support it.'
- 'It's a typical glib presentation. Lots of pictures and noise and I can't get to grips with the change that is wanted so I don't think it will work.'
- 'What is wrong with what we have already been doing?'
- The change is just like all the other initiatives that we've seen – and they have all failed.'
- 'A superb and clear presentation. I can see exactly the way to success.'

Claudia was disappointed in the response. Her message was meant to be inspirational and visionary and she felt frustrated by the inability of her staff to understand. Her managers echoed her frustration for they had run follow-up sessions for the staff using her presentation and they had received similar feedback from their staff.

The Leadership Communication Model

'Contrary to what most chieftain's think you are not remembered by what you did in the past, but by what most think you did.'

Robert Weiss, *'Leadership Secrets of Attila the Hun'*

Claudia will be able to understand much of what happened to her message if she understands the Leadership Communication Model. The model explains the processes of how messages are *deleted*, *generalized* and *distorted*, and how you experience something inside yourself and how *internal representations* of events are created. That you create an internal representation is why the phrase 'it makes me feel down' may create a negative state in you and may also physically make you down. The Leadership Communication Model, shown in Figure 11, is circular. The *external event* causes the *internal representation*, a meaningful pattern which causes the recipient to behave in a certain way in the external world, which then affects the behaviour of the initial sender – that influences a further *external event* for the receiver of the communication.

The stages in the Leadership Communication Model are: An external event occurs. The receiver uses their *senses* – eyes (visual), ears (auditory) and feeling (kinesthetic) – to process the *external* event. The feeling senses include taste (gustatory) and smells (olfactory).

Psychological and communication research since the 1950s has shown us that there are so many external stimuli we can hardly begin to count them. Nevertheless our senses are remarkable and have enough receptors to take in about 11 million bits per second of information. Our conscious capacity to process information, however, is comparatively limited at 40 bits per second. An enormous reduction that demonstrates that most of the detailed data is deleted, distorted and generalized before conscious processing occurs.

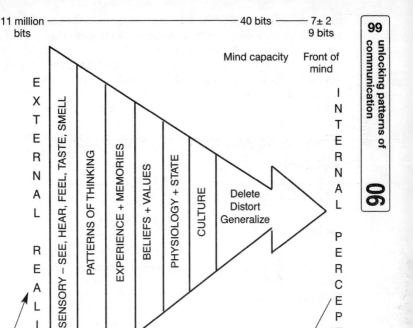

figure 11 leadership communication model

EXERCISE: Tuning in

Do this exercise now. Remember and write down what you heard in the last minute. Now listen really carefully for the next minute and write down things you hear. The second list will be longer than the first. You may now notice sounds outside, a car, a lawnmower or inside, a tap running, a slight noise from the lights that you had previously deleted. If you do this in a group you will be amazed at the different things listed. You realize how much you normally delete from your conciousness so you can begin to make sense of the world. You may repeat the exercise for seeing and feeling.

In 1956 Miller conducted an experiment that showed the limit on the capacity of our conscious brain. He demonstrated that the conscious mind could only hold in seven plus/minus two chunks of data. So how do we remember the UK's 13-digit telephone number? You break the number into pieces – say, national code, area code, and number. Then link it to someone's name and then by linking to the name and once habituated, you store the number in the unconscious brain. Now the conscious brain can focus on other matters. When you need the number you can recall it by linking the name to the number. So to deal with the data you need to remember, the brain takes the new data, and the telephone number and creates a pattern that can become habitual.

Deletion

We delete much of what is available to us. Think of the last book or novel, before this one, that you read. Check if you can answer these questions.

• What did the cover look like?
• What was the exact title?
• Who were the authors?
• Who was the publisher?
• How many chapters were there?
• Who were the main characters?
• What happened on page 12?
• What was the print size?
• What was on the back cover?
• What exactly was the cover like, that you recalled first – colours, pictures, diagrams?

You may argue that much of that data is not relevant, not important and you may be right. They may be not important – to you, the individual, at this time. If you were a publisher or an author you may attend to the production details. If you needed to reference the book or read other books by the same authors, you would attend to the authors' names.

Remember the last report that you read – can you recall all the detail of the arguments made? If not, can you remember the conclusions – exactly? You recognize deletion at work. For instance, when at a meeting someone says as they leave, 'Give me a call about the new project on Wednesday in the afternoon. We need to discuss the costings, the equipment profile, the potential demand and the potential suppliers, particularly the choice between Jones, Smith and Williams. My internal number is 87642 and my email is …'. The next morning you go, 'I must call – who was that? When? Afternoon or morning?' When there is too much data for you to remember precisely you take some action to record it – write it down or stop and create ways of remembering parts. For example, you think Smith and Jones are a comedy duo, so that's the supplier. And if you remember Smith and Jones, it's likely that Williams will pop out.

There is also overload in the communication described above. The conscious mind only comfortably attends to 7 ± 2 stimuli, so it is unlikely that all the detail would be recalled. A memorable communication is, 'Phone me tomorrow afternoon about the project. Please have details on suppliers Jones, Smith and Williams'; six pieces of data that may be remembered. And the communicator decides what 7 ± 2 items are important and gives that data. It is not the listener's job to wade through the morass of data and decide what the communicator believes important in the message. As a leader be specific about your most important messages rather than give every detail of every message.

Generalization

As well as deletion, you generalize to make sense of the world by putting events into classifications or categories. When the event or part of it seems to happen again you jump to the conclusion that it is going to be just like last time. For example 'I once met a mathematician who was boring. Here is another mathematician, he must be boring too.'

A generalization is when you say 'that's one of those, so I will think of it as if it was one of those'. Examples of generalization are:

Experience	Generalization
He's a salesman.	He's like all salesmen.
That's a technology company.	One technology company I know is innovative. It must be innovative.
He's over 65.	He's too old. He won't be computer literate.
He has created a mission statement.	He must be a leader. Leaders create mission statements.
He lost an argument.	He can't be a leader. People who lose arguments aren't leaders.

You do not need to explore cause and effect in the statements above. How the generalization is created is interesting but not critical. What is important is that there is a generalization created. Why you treat the over-65 as computer illiterate is not important. That you do, whether it is true or not, is the effect of the generalization and the effect may be that he/she feels undervalued and demeaned even though he/she is computer literate. And because they feel undervalued they may not contribute as much as they could.

Distortion

We also make sense of our worlds by altering and distorting things to make our own meaning of them.

A common form of distortion that you know from childhood is the message whispered one-to-one around a group. With each whisper a small part of the content is distorted. Not so much that the two who whisper believe they do not understand the message, as to understand the message you do not need all the words. And at the end of the circle 'send reinforcements we're going to advance' has become 'send three and four pence, we are going to a dance' (three and four pence is a sum of money in pre-1971 British currency).

Distortion is evident when the police take statements from an incident. People notice different things depending on the filter that they use, as discussed below. The effect is that the evidence often becomes: 'it was a van', 'a truck', 'a pick-up truck' and it was 'red', 'black' or…. Each individual has a different internal representation of the event. All are true to them.

We also make distortions through mind-reading, where we attribute assumptions, interpretations and meanings without checking out the validity, e.g. 'You don't like me'; 'I know he was happy with what we did'; 'My partner will never agree to move office so I won't even ask'. A leader should challenge these distortions by asking: 'How do you know I don't like you?'; 'What evidence leads you to believe he was happy with us?'; 'How do you know that your partner will not move? You have moved twice before have you not?'

Distortions give us shortcuts in language and yet sometimes they are actually short-circuits and cause us to make faulty and unhelpful linkages. We often have short-circuits between 'cause and effect'. For example, 'you make me angry'. Clarifying this you could ask, 'how does my behaviour cause you to choose to be angry?'

A third common distortion is when we think one thing equals another, called complex equivalence: e.g. 'You didn't put the rubbish out, you don't care about me'; 'He didn't stay late means he is not committed to the company'. Leaders can get clarity by unpicking the equation and asking 'How does not putting the rubbish out equal me not caring about you?' and 'How specifically does him not staying late mean he us uncaring about the company?' The effect of one small distortion can cause a much deeper disagreement.

Have you ever had the experience where at a meeting you meet someone who looks, behaves and talks like a colleague? You distort such that you treat this person as if he was that colleague – and grant the unknown person the positive qualities of the colleague – without any evidence, and are surprised when the now 'colleague' does not treat you like the existing colleague.

How do you delete, generalize and distort?

You delete, generalize and distort because you can't take in with accuracy everything you experience. You *filter* the external event to allow you to make sense of it. The filters are:

Patterns of thinking

How you sort, orient, or scale your experiences. As an example of what is termed *a pattern of thinking*, some people always look for the benefits of a change, the enjoyment of reaching goals, whereas others always look for the pitfalls and what could go wrong. Their internal response affects whether they are positive or negative in how they respond to change. These important thinking patterns are discussed further in Chapter 7, but you can already recognize how they affect the way a communication is received.

Personal experience and memories

What has happened to you before. If you hear a 'bang' as you are driving, and you have had a blowout in the last week, you are likely to have an internal representation of fear, or concern and the memory of the flat tyre, and that causes you to pull over more quickly. Someone who was an inexperienced driver may distort the sound, not hearing it for what it is, drive on and, if it was a blowout, ruin the tyre. The staff member who says that 'this change is like all the initiatives we've seen' will be working from her experience.

Belief and values

Beliefs are the generalizations you make about the world, your operating principles about causality, meaning and others' behaviour and identity. They are your own rule sets about what is right or wrong, possible or not possible. You explored Churchill's belief in Chapter 5. You understand how altering a belief changes how you deal with external experiences. The 'clever' trainees do better than the 'normal' trainees – yet they are subjected to the same external stimulus, the training. Your beliefs come from many sources – upbringing, modelling of significant others, and past experience. Beliefs are what you believe to be 'fine' at the moment. Values in a wider sense are what is important to us and are supported by our beliefs. Values are what motivate you in life. At some level they drive what you do. Values relate your identity, as discussed in logical levels in Chapter 5. You really care about them. They are the fundamental principles you operate by. Values are explored further in Chapter 10. You can imagine how holding different values would cause people to distort, delete and generalize in different ways. The difference between values and beliefs can be seen in Churchill. Churchill's father died when he was very young. Churchill had the value that doing as much as possible in the time available is very important. The belief was that there is not much time to get work done as I, too, may die young and so, when I have work to do, I need to get on with it immediately.

Language

You can give different meanings for words that alter the internal representation. You use the word 'challenge' to describe a project. A 'challenge' to one person may mean a threat. To another it may be an opportunity to excel. The response from the individual will depend on their view – whether they reject or welcome the new project. How you can use language precisely and artfully is explored further in Chapters 7 and 8.

Culture

The same behaviours may have different meaning depending on the culture of an organization or community, or the cultural background of an individual. Culture derives from a complex interaction of values and beliefs. Language, common practice and gestures within a community reinforce culture. Unwritten laws apply. The gesture 'O' with the thumb and forefinger can mean OK in a British culture. In an Italian culture it is rude. In Britain, if you say 'yes', you nod the head up and down. In

Greece, the head is moved from side to side. This difference is confusing to a Briton, as side to side is connected to 'no' in Britain.

Senses

The senses are how you perceive the external events – sight, sound, feel, smell, or taste. You each have differently developed senses. People with a highly developed auditory sense are more likely to respond to sounds that the less developed will not hear. The same picture of a lake to someone with highly developed visual sense may be bright and panoramic with deep colours. To the less visually developed it may look like a blue flat sea. The same external event has a different internal representation and a different importance in how they interpret and make sense of the world around them.

To illustrate, three people meet in the bar after a fraught change strategy meeting. The participant with a highly developed auditory sense may recall more of the phrases used, including those whispered 'off-stage'. The 'visual' will have a clear picture of who sat where, the gestures people made, and the colours and design of the PowerPoint presentation. The 'kinesthetic' manager will access their recall through their emotion and feeling about the event, and through the emotion and feeling of others at the meeting. All can recall visual, auditory and kinesthetic events and for each of the three, the richest source of recall is their preferred sense.

Communication using the senses

How people talk about an event afterwards reflects their preferred sense for coding external events. Visual people say things like, 'I got a clear picture', 'you can see what she was saying', and 'she made her vision clear to me'. Auditory people might say, 'I heard his central points loud and clear', 'his ideas resonate with me', and 'he was clear as a bell'. A kinesthetic person might say, 'I could really empathize', 'he feels deeply about his ideas', and 'he is passionate about expressing them'.

There is no agreement about the percentage breakdown of preferred representational systems in the population. According to Bodenhauser and Hall, 60 per cent are 'visual', 20 per cent are 'auditory' and 20 per cent are 'kinesthetic'. But for Molder, 35 per cent are 'visual', 20 per cent are 'auditory' and 45 per cent are 'kinesthetic'. But what is 'clear' (appeals to the visual and auditory both) is that if you stay and communicate in just one representation system and use words that describe just that representation system you can miss out many of the audience to whom you wish to appeal. What is important is that you need to use language that draws from a range of representational systems for your audience, so they can all connect with what you are saying.

While this breakdown of three sensory systems is widely believed, Johnson described the results as a 'myth', as the research that gave the results above was based on exploring the emotions behind a single word. Johnson makes the point that 'if you have ever played charades, you know that words and language are by far the most effective way of expressing complex and abstract ideas'. But the words and all **three** are interrelated and important for effective and powerful senses communication.

You now know that 7 per cent of meaning comes from the words, 38 per cent from the voice and 55 per cent from the body: body and voice speak volumes (the 93 per cent) while words speak pages (the 7 per cent). The key to communication is the 93 per cent (the how) rather than the 7 per cent (the what). When you say 'Thank you' how often have you noticed someone's eyes, voice, or facial expression communicates that they appreciated the help you had given them? Or that they do not appreciate your 'thank you', and wish you would go away. It is critical that you ensure that your messages are delivered with congruence using the 93 per cent.

The internal representation: the consequences of the deletions, generalizations and distortions

'A Hun's perception is reality to him.'
Robert Weiss, *The Leadership Secrets of Attila the Hun*

The consequence of the process of deletion, generalization and distortion creates a unique representation, an internal representation, of the world built on the individual's patterns, thinking, personal experience and memories, belief and values, language – cultural experience and senses.

The internal representation will differ between individuals. A story about spiders produces a different reaction in the arachnaphobe, compared with the spider expert. Staff watching Claudia present get different internal representations from her words. Some see her as competent, others as confusing.

Therefore, when asked to comment on her presentation they give different responses: 'excellent, knows where she is going' or 'woolly, unclear, doesn't know what she's at'. Yet both have had the same external experience – that of the presentation.

For any given external experience, we each generate different 'maps' that contain the bits that we notice, with our unique deletions, generalizations and distortions. The concept of 'maps' can be expanded to give you an insight into the way others view the world, and how individual's maps affect what they perceive in the external world.

A useful analogy is that of a map. When you are interested in looking for a road, you would use a road map – but that road map would not tell you where the buildings were. And if you got the map of historic bars in a city, it would show some of the roads, but it might not show the church that you wish to find. And if you use a map with the scale one centimetre to the kilometre, you might be able to see the route from A to B but it won't show the houses and landmarks that a larger scale map would. And if you wanted to see the house with the red door or the hole in the road you would need a map that was the same size as the world you were exploring – an impractical proposition.

The effect of individuals' 'maps' gives rise to different responses. If a team is visiting another business, the accountant may experience issues the marketing people don't experience, and vice versa. We all have different 'maps' and yet often assume that there is only one 'map' – ours, and often argument is about forcing others to accept the 'truth' of our own map. So you must ask with your understanding of maps – is there a true map?

Understanding that you and your followers store 'maps' not the reality is a key to successful leadership communication, and is contained in possibly the most powerful presupposition – *'the map is not the territory'*. What you experience is not the total reality.

As you say the words in the exercise (over page), note your internal representation, your mood and any changes to your body. The experience is filtered to create an internal representation that is uplifting and inspirational. Your mood lifts, you feel inspired by the nobility of the human spirit and you may believe that you too can achieve your dreams – you may have noticed your chest lift, your breathing quicken, and your head and eyes lift. The sensation may be greater if you have

EXERCISE: Internal representation – and its links with state and physiology

Experience the words of Martin Luther King. Imagine you are talking to a rapt audience. Say the words – out loud if possible – with feeling:

'I have a dream that one day this nation will rise up, live to the true meaning of its creed: we hold these truths to be self-evident that all men are created equal.'

Martin Luther King, Washington, August 1963

had experience of the civil rights movement or even seen movies depicting the struggle. You will have noticed that the internal representation has affected your mood and body. The three areas are doubly interconnected. *Internal representation* will affect *state* and *physiology*. We described how *internal representation* affects *state* and *state* affects *physiology*. All affect each other interdependently, as you will experience in the next exercise.

Self-exercise

Look down with your head slumped and eyes focused on the ground. Now remember a time when you felt really successful, really good and keep looking down, with your head slumped.

You may have found looking down a difficult posture to maintain while having such positive thoughts. Usually when you are physiologically down, your state is a down one, and your internal representation will often be negative. A successful leader we know says 'lift' when she needs to be in a positive state . She changes her body posture to head high and shoulders square. She changes from a negative or neutral state to a positive one. This change affects her and it certainly affects those around her.

You can come up with your own way to be able to lift your physiology, stance and internal dialogue.

Self-talk

Self-talk is the final part of the leadership communication model that affects your state. So far the model has considered only external events that you filter. You can also generate 'internal representations' from inside yourself. *Self-talk* or internal dialogue, the voice that often chats away to us, also affects the other three systems of sight, sound and feelings. The little voice saying 'I can do this', 'I can't do this', 'what if this happened?', 'I feel really down today' will affect all three systems. One other effect of *self-talk* is that it can block your awareness of external events. Indeed if your *self-talk* is saying 'what a strange thing – surely people don't talk to themselves or do they?' you may need to re-read the last paragraph to check which words and meaning you missed. The self-talk has blocked your sensing of the external event. The tonality and volume of your self-talk can also affect state. A sleepy internal voice saying 'I'm tired' will create weariness. A voice saying 'I'm energetic and I will do this' will bring you to life.

The leader's behaviour

The leader's *behaviour* is the outcome of the interplay between *self-talk*, *state*, *internal representation*, and *physiology*. This behaviour is seen in the external world and influences a response from the external world which is then sensed – and the cycles of *behaviour* affecting *behaviour* begin.

The cycles are often reinforcing. If the external event starts positively, with the leader's communication indicating that the follower can complete the task, the follower will pick up on the many cues given – words, body actions, and voice tone. The follower is likely to give a more positive response, and is more likely to generate the *behaviours* that will create a positive response in the leader. The leader has created a virtuous circle.

On the other hand you could begin by saying 'I'm not too sure if you can do this' with a hesitant voice tone, downbeat tones, and you will get a more negative response – you may have created a debilitating circle leading to lower performance. The leader needs to use all three elements of communication – remembered as the verse (words), the song (tonality) and dance (body) of communication.

Case analysis

Claudia the CEO did not receive the positive response she expected to her declaration of the mission statement. We can explore possible flaws through analysis using the leadership communication model. Key points are:

- The use of PowerPoint and words appeals to the visual and auditory. There was little kinesthetic component.
- The CEO may not have been congruent in her presentation. It is possible that her state, and thus her behaviour, was affected by the late night in preparation of the presentation. Her tiredness and nervousness may have shone through (a metaphor that works best with the visual).
- Her message may have been filtered differently by staff. Some staff see 'challenge' as very threatening while others find it 'a great opportunity'. Some were looking for what is good. Some looked for what is bad about her statements. They have different patterns of thinking.
- Some staff perceive their previous experience and memory on initiatives that have not been supported and judge as a generalization that this one will also fail.

Communication is complex, as complex as each individual with whom you communicate. You need to be aware, as is stated in another presupposition of leadership that *'the meaning of any communication is the response you get'*. If you are aware of this presupposition you will accept that your communication has not failed, rather you have some feedback where the receiver has interpreted the meaning differently, and you will then, in the nature of the communication cycle, do something differently to get the message over. The key is that you remain aware of others' communication, and that you listen to what is expressed and the way it is expressed.

EXERCISE: Using the senses to communicate exceptionally

You have already discussed the three sensory systems – visual, auditory and kinesthetic – through which you acquire information. A useful first step to deeper understanding and use of these systems is to understand better your own preferences. These preferences combine to create your thinking strategy.

The Representational System Preference Test

For each of the following statements, please place a number next to every phrase. Use the following system to indicate your preferences for each of the statements:

4 = closest to describing you
3 = next best description
2 = third best
1 = least descriptive of you

1 I make important decisions based on:
  a _____ how I feel, what is comfortable.
  b _____ which way sounds best.
  c _____ what appears best to me.
  d _____ detailed analysis of the key facts.
2 During a debate, I am most likely to be influenced by:
  a _____ someone's tone of voice.
  b _____ how the other's argument appears.
  c _____ the logic of the other person's argument.
  d _____ how I feel about the other person's feelings.
3 I most easily communicate what is going on with me by:
  a _____ my appearance, my clothes and my demeanor.
  b _____ my feelings shared with others.
  c _____ my language and words.
  d _____ the tone, timbre and pitch of my speech.
4 I find it easier to:
  a _____ select the volume and tuning on a hi-fi system.
  b _____ analyse and synthesize key aspects of a relevant issue.
  c _____ choose the most comfortable clothes.
  d _____ choose colour schemes for a room.
5 I operate best:
  a _____ aware of the sounds around me.
  b _____ making sense of facts and data.
  c _____ comfortable with the feelings of those around me.
  d _____ seeing that things fit into the picture.

Scoring the Representational Preference Test

1 Take your response to each question, and place the response in the table below. If you responded (**a**) in Question **1** your rating goes in the column Kinesthetic. Complete for the five scores.

	Visual	Kinesthetic	Auditory	Auditory Digital
Q1	(c)	(a)	(b)	(d)
Q2	(b)	(d)	(a)	(c)
Q3	(a)	(b)	(d)	(c)
Q4	(d)	(c)	(a)	(b)
Q5	(d)	(c)	(a)	(b)
Total				

2 Total your scores in each column.

You have answered five questions that reveal an indication of your preferences. If you scored 4 in any column that would indicate that for each question you believe that this description was 'closest to describing you'. If you scored 0 for each response in a column you would five times have believed that the preference was 'least descriptive of you'. It is unlikely that you will have scored each question the same. The totals though give an indication of your analysis of your preference.

Please transfer your total score to this rank. You now know your preference.

Score

Highest score	– First preference	is	_____
2nd highest score	– Second preference	is	_____
3rd highest score	– Third preference	is	_____
Lowest score	– lowest preference	is	_____

You will see we have added an additional preference that is a product of self-talk: AD refers to Auditory Digital – the internal words that you form from sound. The digital (on/off) means that the words have an exact meaning to the individual – i.e. there are no shades of meaning in 'precise review' in the way that there can be brightness, colour, or haziness that what looks best to me can have.

You now have an understanding of your preferred representational system. A check is to explore your use of language when you present. Claudia, the CEO in the case study, chose to 'reveal a picture' of the mission statement that she wished to present. Her choice of language reveals that she may have a visual primary representational system. By **only** using visual language she did not connect with those in her audience who have an auditory or kinesthetic representational system. Other 'visual' words she may use, that are clues to her others' representational systems, are:

Focus	See	Clear
Bright	Picture	Perspective
Show	Hazy	Colourful
Pretty	Glimpse	Illustrate
Outlook	Depict	Paint
Dress up	Reveal	

If she had asked her audience to 'listen – our mission is loud and clear', she would be revealing that her primary system is auditory. Other auditory clues are:

Listen	Say	Talk
Harmony	Noisy	Discuss
Call	Loud	Shout
Told	Voice	Muffle
Click	Ask	Tone
Screech	Hear	

She could also have told the audience that 'she was going to lay her cards on the table – the new mission statement will create a firm foundation for the business'. This statement reveals a liking for the kinesthetic preference. Other words that reveal the kinesthetic preference are:

Feel	Firm	Touch
Pressure	Tense	Concrete
Hurt	Movement	Irritable
Clumsy	Pushy	Sharpen
Strike	Grope	Rub
Stroke	Sore	

There are other words that would reveal the more precise kinesthetic olfactory/gustatory preferences. These are words like:

Bitter	Smell	Stale
Fragrant	Sour	Sweet
Fresh		

The Auditory Digital phase uses a neutral representational system. Use of these phrases does not reveal the individual's primary representational system. You need to listen further to gain the information on the primary representational system.

Analyse
Change
Conceive
Experience
Perceive
Question
Understand

Aware
Code
Decide
Know
Process
Sense

Be conscious
Consider
Distinct
Learn
Identify
Think

Analysis of case study: representational systems

In this case study, Claudia should have used a range of representation phases to get her message over so she would appeal to all of her audience:

• She could 'paint a picture' of the future adding colours and brightness to the picture that is the mission, and let people see how it would be in reality.

• She could clearly express the message creating the 'sound of success' and 'voice in detail' of the mission statement.

• She could create a warm feeling and 'lay her cards on the table' such that all could get 'a handle on' the new mission and invite people to be comfortable and relaxed about implementing it.

EXERCISE

People will tell you their preferred representation system through their language and it is easy to spot. Say the following phrases that could happen in any discussion and note whether they are Visual, Auditory, Kinesthetic (include feeling), Olfactory, Gustatory or non-specific. Then you can have fun, spotting the way real people use language to indicate their preferred thinking pattern.

1 I want you to get a grasp of this.
2 I can see what you mean.
3 He has a blind spot.
4 It was a ding dong row.
5 I've no experience of that issue.
6 I need a hand with this project.
7 I understand the analysis.
8 We have to recognize his point of view.
9 It's important to maintain a sense of balance.
10 He's always shouting the odds.

11 Longer term we must create harmony.

12 It's important to sense how things have changed.

Answers:

(1) kinesthetic, (2) visual, (3) visual, (4) auditory, (5) non-specific, (6) kinesthetic, (7) non-specific, (8) visual, (9) kinesthetic, (10) auditory, (11) auditory, (12) non-specific.

Clearer perspectives give clearer meaning for leaders

There are even more ways to understand how to communicate effectively as a leader. In this section, you consider how to extend the perception of leaders.

Claudia has now begun to realize that the employees had filtered her message such that her message had been *deleted*, *distorted* and *generalized*. She could have anticipated many of these difficulties by analysing the effect her presentation would have from differing perspectives, i.e. from differing *perceptual positions*. You can operate from three basic ways of looking at experience that offer tremendous potential for extending insight and improving communication. You create more wisdom for leaders, by increasing perception of others' patterns of thinking, personal experiences, memories, beliefs and values, language and culture, and the senses. The perceptual positions can be described as follows:

- First perceptual position (the *I* position): You see the world from your own point of view, and from your own reality within yourself. You simply think 'how does this issue or communication affect me?' You actually fully experience how you feel about this. The state you are in is known as being 'associated' into your experience.

- Second position (the *you* position): you process the experience from the position of the other person. You take into account how the experience would be from the other person's point of view. You see, hear, and feel the world from the other's position. You also imagine their beliefs, values and thinking. In this state you 'associate' with the other person's reality.

- Third position (the *they* position): you move to an uninvolved position, as someone who is outside the situation. You are an independent observer. You ask yourself 'how would this event be experienced by someone totally uninvolved?' Perhaps as if they were watching a wide view movie filmed from high up. This is a way of analysing from a detached view what is happening. In this position you are 'disassociated' and emotion free.

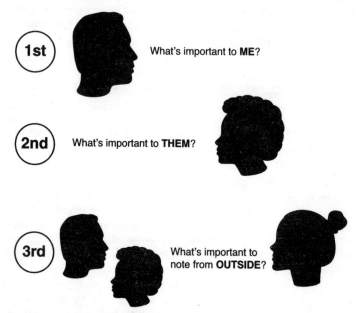

figure 12 perceptual positions

One way of understanding these perceptional positions is to think of the three roles as shown below:

- In first position – I am in a hole
- In second position – someone comes and jumps in with you – and empathizes with your position
- In third position – someone comes along, sees what is really happening and calmly finds a rope and pulls you out (and possibly the other person).

If you become stuck in any one of the three positions the following may happen:

A person stuck:	Becomes:
In first position	egotistical
In second position	a rescuer, caretaker
In third position	cold and unfeeling

A person stuck in *first position* only perceives issues from their position. In *second position*, the person is constantly over-influenced by other people's views, and lets the state of others determine their state. They become co-dependent. They are not in control of their own state. In *third position* a person becomes detached and unfeeling. They may become the loners of the world, detached and unable to relax on a human level.

Effective actors are known for their rich ability to step into the shoes of their characters and become that person, to move into second position. Meryl Streep is famed for the impact she makes by taking the body posture, language and values of her characters. She becomes that person for a period, fully associated. Gandhi wrote that when he prepared for negotiation he would consider situations as a Hindu, Muslim, and British. He thought of specific individuals and would adapt their body positions to become fully associated with second position and to gain greater understanding of their position. In one particular instance he walked around the house holding his hands like the Briton with whom he was going to negotiate. Gandhi was also able to imagine being disassociated and in third position by imagining he was the World Service of the BBC reporting on his proposed ideas.

To understand and learn the most from any experience you need to gather as many new viewpoints as possible because everyone has their own *map of the world*, their internal representation. If you develop the skill of sensing differing maps you will have additional information to see through your blind spots. Use of the three positions broadens your awareness and perspective on a problem, gives you greater choice, and if you choose to exercise your choices, greater flexibility – and another presupposition of success as a leader, the person with *the greatest flexibility* is in *control of the situation*.

Case analysis

In the presentation of her mission statement, Claudia may have considered the presentation from first position: she was excited about the mission statement – after all she had developed it. She had worked until the early hours to prepare the presentation and it was good – for her. But it didn't work. If she had gone to second position, she could have asked the question 'If I was them, what would they hear, see and feel as they sit through this presentation? What would they want to hear, see, and feel? What emotions do they see me portraying? – Do I look tired to them? How do I sound to them?' and thus experience how others reacted to her work. For example:

- The person who said 'change makes me feel down' – from second position Claudia could have anticipated that change would challenge as it probably had before. She could emphasize the continuity in 'developing and building on our own values'.

- 'All other initiatives have failed' – This is likely to have been said before by this person. From first position Claudia believes that the initiative won't fail. Consciously using her view from this position, she cannot use the word initiative and turn it into 'building on past work in this area'.

Looking at how her presentation might be experienced from third position, Claudia would see the visual impact of her PowerPoint presentation, and hear her words – and recognizes that there is little for the kinesthetic person. Perhaps she could add some part to her presentation that people could handle and feel – for the kinesthetic there is meaning when there is an opportunity to feel and touch a representation of the vision.

At times you may also find it useful to gain additional information, an even wider perspective, an 'out there' position. In this position, you consider what would be in the interest of the whole system. How would Claudia's mission statement look to the whole hospitality industry – other hotels and tourist bodies?

An artistic view

We had the opportunity to interview David McCallister, the Artistic Director of the Australian Ballet Company. David moved into this leadership role directly from being a Principal Dancer. We were motivated to talk to him having heard him speak eloquently about valuing different perspectives within the company.

We asked him what really mattered to him (First Position) about taking up the role of Artistic Director. He replied:

'I guess what really mattered to me was actually looking at how this organization *could* be. As Artistic Director I have to straddle both camps, of dancers and administration, and I guess, coming from being a dancer, I sort of thought OK how can I bring the dancers' perspective into the administration of this company and vice versa. I had to actually try and mould what I knew about administration and look at it in the way the dancers could work into their world. So my aim was to try and bridge the gap. Not that there is a huge gap but try and be the conduit everyone could use to work more effectively together. I wanted to really try and create an environment for everyone in the organization who is involved in this artistic pursuit to actually feel they can fly, be creative and be the best they possibly can be.'

From first position we asked: 'What's the most powerful thing that motivates you?' David responded:

'I have such a passion for this art form I just love it. I get motivated when I see people develop and the most scary thing I do is handing out the opportunity. Casting and commissioning work; that is the biggest risk and the biggest challenge, but then the biggest excitement is when people you engage either as dancers or choreographers, then come up with a piece of work which is just incredibly beautiful. That inspires me and motivates me to come in each day and to get the best possible resources. Another astounding thing, I thought that when I took over this job it would be up to me to generate all the ideas, but in fact what I've found is all these amazing people with fantastic ideas and you actually just have to put the right people together and they generate a whole lot of creative ideas. What I have to do is choose the ones that are going to go at this particular time.'

We then asked, from the Dancers' perspective, 'If you were in their shoes, what would be important to you as a dancer? What happens when you second position them?' David said:

'I would say to have challenges, to have new things to stimulate. Now, as a dancer I'd probably say I'd like a little bit of time off because lots of different things have been thrown in. Dancers always want to excel, we always want to develop, we want challenges either repertoire based, physically or teaching, so we become a greater artist. I would want to be stimulated and be constantly developing. I would love to have more to develop either a role or a character or to really get my teeth stuck into a technical challenge within a ballet, and there's always that thing "oh I wish we had another week of rehearsal, that would be even better", but I think that the element of being challenged as well as having the time to achieve those challenges would be the thing that I think the dancers would really love to have.'

Finally we asked David to stand outside that dynamic, in third position, and have a look at what's happening and almost float above it and disconnect his feelings so that he can take a colder look at it.

He replied: 'Yeah it's quite fascinating actually because I'm sitting here looking at the make up of the year's schedule and how it sits together and it's interesting because as well as thinking "Is this going to challenge the dancers? Is this going to make sense? Is this going to work as a schedule in relation to what's going to develop them?" I'm also thinking: Is there an audience for this? Is this a programme that an audience would want to see? I'm seeing the ballet goer, do they look as if they want to see this? Does it fit together? Is there a sense of reason behind the balance? I guess most of the time, you try and be really analytic and go "yes I think I can see that or I think that's a bit heavy on the new work or a bit heavy on the old stuff", I need to think about how the whole artistic balance will look when I reflect back on my time at the helm.'

OK David, so if you were to go all the way back to you being you and feeling how you feel about the role and if you had to give yourself one piece of advice from yourself to yourself, from that first position, what would your piece of advice be?

'Never be scared to just say what you think, to be honest without being evil – really say what you think.'

Good. And then if you were then in the dancers' shoes, so you being them, second position, and giving yourself one piece of advice, what would you say?

'"Be a little less wishy washy." It's good to have people to give you a voice but then I think sometimes there comes a time to make a decision and I think they would say "you need to be more decisive sometimes".'

So then just floating above all of that and watching you interacting with the dancers and the audience and all your wider connections, from this third position, looking at the dynamic and seeing you in there, what would be the piece of advice from out here that you would give to yourself?

'I think what I would say to myself is 'actually listen and then go with your gut instinct.' And, 'Don't talk too much when other people are trying to tell you stuff and listen to what they are saying and then make a decision. Don't make a decision then try and talk everyone into it.'

EXERCISE

If you have the ability to move cleanly between the perceptual positions, consciously or unconsciously, you can act with greater wisdom and appreciate the complexity of what is happening – and when you understand the complexity you have more choice. None of the positions is superior to the other. Most of us naturally spend more time in one of the three positions – first, second and third. The differing perspectives help you to understand any situation better and know 'reality' more fully. Use of 'perceptual positions' allows you quickly to get to the key filters that affect your and others' behaviour.

This exercise is designed to give you practice in the development of choices.

Recall a recent argument that you had with someone where the outcome was not what you wanted. Now go through the three perceptual positions:

First position: Associate into the experience you had then by seeing what you saw, hearing what you heard and feeling what you felt. On a sheet of paper, note how you now feel, and the insights you now have. Note the advice you would give to yourself from this perspective.

Second position: Now step out of your own experience and into the body and experience of the other person. Assume the beliefs, values and perspectives of the other person. Note how from their eyes you must have looked during the argument. What tone of voice did you use? How do you feel as you watch yourself speak? Note the insights you get from this position, and again the advice you would give to yourself from this second position.

Third position: Now come away from the other person's experience and disassociate from your own, drift to a third position where you are disassociated from the event. If you find yourself drawn back to first or second perceptual position because of the energy of the argument, imagine a glass wall between you and the other two involved in the argument. Note how you view the argument, and again note the advice you would give to yourself from this detached position.

Compare the notes you have made. Notice how your reactions and feelings and insights have differed in each position. Has your perception of the argument changed? Would you have given a different response to the person had you done this during the argument?

If you have identified different responses you now have the capability to discover more choices in communication, and if you choose to be flexible, have more options open to you and – as you recall – the person with the most flexibility has the most influence over the system.

Learning for leadership success

We have explored how we access our experience in the external world to create realities, maps, for ourselves that influenced our behaviour. Our behaviour influences the external world that we then experience to set up the cycle of leadership communication. We then discussed the filters used to distort, delete and generalize. The filters are:

- Patterns of motivation and thinking – meta-programmes
- Deletions, distortions and generalizations
- Personal experience and memories
- Beliefs and values
- Language
- Culture
- Senses and
- Preference for different types of words.

The techniques that allow us to understand others better are:

- Communication using the senses – using visual, auditory and kinesthetic senses creates compelling images.
- The three perspectives – how you can gain amazing insights into others' maps by second and third positioning.

Reflection

Final thought on communicating as a leader. It was really interesting talking with you. It has provoked all sorts of thoughts about the way I think. Thinking about yourself in the context of yourself is really quite fascinating. As a dancer I was always one of those people that was so easily motivated I was looking for someone to tell me all the time what they thought of me and where I could get better and all that sort of stuff. You always wait for the teachers at the front of the room to correct you or you look in the mirror to look for what you have got to do. I think sometimes we lose track of ourselves and how we can coach and advise ourselves if there is always a coach at the front of the room, if there is always a ballet teacher.

And thinking about things from someone else's viewpoint. It's something I thought when I took over this job, 'Don't forget don't forget don't forget, always remember what it's like to be a dancer' because at the end of the day, that's the most important thing. It's so easy to now go 'I wouldn't have done that, I wouldn't have been kicking up this fuss', and you just have to keep going 'no, no stop it'. And it's always that other thing too like, 'Oh they think they're working hard, well they should hear what I've got to do' but that doesn't matter because they are not the artistic director, they're the dancers and what they're doing is working really hard as a dancer.

And finally, *be prepared to be judged by your legacy.*

David McAllister

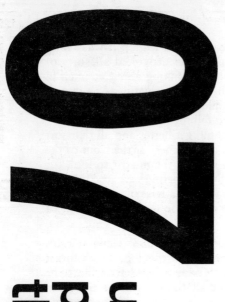

07
unlocking patterns of thinking

In this chapter you will:
- understand five frequently found thinking patterns
- use the thinking patterns to understand and influence followers

'We must have strong minds ready to accept facts as they are.'

Harry S. Trueman

'Honest differences are often a healthy sign of progress.'

Mahatma Gandhi

Introduction

This chapter will explore what causes different *patterns of thinking* in people. These patterns are also called *meta-programs*. By understanding this you can gain insight into how it may appear that people are 'wired' in different ways; how it is that one person's fascination may be another's boredom; how one's 'clear process' can be another's 'straitjacket'. As a leader of others, recognition of your own patterns of thinking and motivation can help you develop flexibility. Understanding patterns of motivation in others can hot-wire you to powerful influence and connection to their motivational circuitry or 'meta' programs. Without this understanding often people are labelled as 'weird', 'difficult', or 'on a different planet', rather than simply that they use their thinking pattern to view the world differently. As you remember, *the map is not the territory.*

These differences are due to preferences in patterns of thinking rather than being difficult. With the understanding of patterns of thinking you can recognize the codes or circuits they use and consequently be able to lock on to their way of processing when you want influence. If you accept the presupposition that *behaviour is not identity*, you can move to the position where what individuals do is only a behaviour, and not a reflection of their identity. And why they do what they do is inspired by their thinking patterns or meta-programs.

Patterns of thinking

'Ask people to talk about what matters to them, not to ask them to support what matters to us.'

Block in *Stewardship*

Powerful filters of how you experience the world are the patterns of thinking, the *meta-programs* that you use. *Meta-programs* are sorting filters. They cause us to put our attention in certain places and not in others. You then develop a habitual pattern in how you think, make decisions and behave. Some people have lots of detail and this detail really helps them understand how everything works and fits together and to know exactly what will happen. If detail is your preference, paragraph A below will match how you think and filter.

> Paragraph A: 'In this section below you will discuss five meta-programs. Examples of the two opposites on the meta-program continuum will be given, with definitions, examples of the behaviours used by each of the two opposites, and suggestions about how you may communicate effectively to people with each preference. You will then apply the program within the case study. You will be given a self-assessment exercise to identify followers' patterns, and to recognize and change your thinking patterns.'

An alternative approach (paragraph B) using the opposite of detail, is to give a big picture:

> Paragraph B: 'At the end of this section you will understand how you can use meta-programs to lead and influence more effectively.'

What you 'think' about issues provides your motivation to act. If you 'think' detail, your actions will focus on the detail of the issue. If you 'think' big picture your actions will focus on how the issue fits with the bigger environment. Often when you say 'he doesn't think like me' it is because he uses different thinking patterns and when you say 'she thinks like me', she uses the same patterns.

Case study

Two high technology companies, Worldlink and Technica, have merged to form WorldlinkTechnica. The Managing Director, Elaine, had spent considerable time thinking about the introductory message to all staff. As you read this statement, you may wish to note what parts have had an impact on you and what parts you do not like:

'With our stockholder's approval and the closing of our merger, WorldlinkTechnica is positioned to realize the full potential of our enhanced scale and global market presence. WorldlinkTechnica product line and extensive engineering resources are second to none in the industry. Our expanded customer support capabilities and world class system level expertise will enable us to offer unmatched individualized market support.

'All of us at WorldlinkTechnica are thrilled with the rapid successful completion of our merger and feel you have today taken a significant step towards fulfilling our vision of becoming the world's premier network systems provider. Our company applies the industry's largest history in network systems research and development, as well as over 12 years' field experience to offer unparalleled customer support.'

Elaine had asked some staff members for feedback, and the comments had been paradoxical. She had used *perceptual position* and the *leadership communication model* to help her in her design of the presentation. She was puzzled at some of the negative comments, as she thought she had covered all of the concerns of her staff. The comments are contained within the following discussion of the five patterns.

Big picture–detail

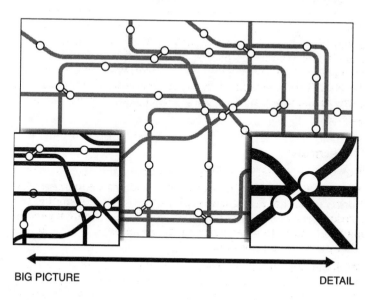

BIG PICTURE   DETAIL

figure 13 the big picture–detail continuum

Paragraphs A and B above, effectively set learning objectives for this chapter. One may have appealed more than the other. Please re-read paragraphs A and B. If A appeals more you may have a preference for Detail. If B appeals you have a preference for Big Picture. Churchill had both the ability to see the big picture and also to work with the detail of an argument.

Big picture

About Elaine's statement, **Safraz** commented: 'It was difficult to make sense of what was being said. The purpose of the merger wasn't made clear.'

Big picture thinkers:

- Are generally convinced by the overall concept. They may miss the detail required
- Concentrate on leading the overall direction of the project/task
- Respond to the big picture first, and then think of the details and specific pieces
- Tend to summarize tasks and events

Tell-tale signs:

- Talk about vision, concepts, and strategy
- Connect one idea to another different idea
- If they get too much detail they will often ask you to come to the point

How to communicate with big picture people:

- Present the big idea first. Limit the details
- Remember, they may fill in the detail of your big idea differently
- Words to use: overall, framework, idea, flexible

Overall, Safraz was very satisfied with Elaine's statement. The notion of 'realize full potential of our enhanced scale and global market presence' worked for him as did the vision of 'become the world's premier network systems provider'.

Detail

However, **Jim** commented about Elaine's statement that: 'There wasn't enough detail to understand the mission statement, and you seemed to jump about from strategy to detail back to strategy without getting to grips with the key points and how can you possibly offer 'unmatched individualized support'? That would require a lot of detailed planning.'

Detail thinkers:

- Break tasks into its parts, often quite small steps
- Focus on detail. The details are needed first, and are required before any decision is made
- Require concrete examples. Sometimes they lose the overall purpose of the task, as they are lost in the detail

Tell-tale signs:

- Talk about 'stages, steps, levels' in a task
- When their train of thought is broken, they go back to the start

How to communicate with detail thinkers:

- Break decisions into parts, and present them in an ordered fashion
- Be specific – ambiguity distracts and confuses them
- Key words: exact, ordered, first, second, third, schedule, breakdown

Jim was clearly unhappy with the detail that was needed. To appeal to Jim, Elaine would have needed to give the detail on how the company was to supply 'unmatched individualized support'. Until Jim has his level of detail met it is unlikely he will fully buy into the pattern. So Elaine should say to appeal to Jim: 'We will plan in detail to provide customer support. The final stage will be a Customer Needs Analysis, the second will be ...'

How do you use both the big picture and detail in a presentation?

'If you talk to a man in a language he understands, that goes to his head. If you talk to him in his language, that goes to his heart.'

Nelson Mandela

Big picture–detail is one of the most important patterns of thinking that you will consider. You will be thinking (at big picture or detail) 'How may I present input using different patterns?' If the presentation is split 50/50 does this mean that 50 per cent of what is said irritates the non-considered thinking pattern? Not really – the listeners are unable to consciously process all of the speech and so what they pay attention to is likely to be their preferred pattern. They delete the bits they don't like! If you included both Elaine's new statements in a presentation, she would have appealed to both preferences – and she may have received comments such as:

Safraz: 'Great vision. I know where we're going. Something will happen about detailed roll out – it's good I'm sure, and I didn't really catch it' (from the big picture thinker who doesn't want the detail anyway).

Jim: 'Excellent that we'll consider the objective of providing customer support at each level and each stage. It all seemed a bit too inspirational and vague – and I know when it's broken down it will make sense' (from the detail thinker).

The key is that you are aware of differing needs and show the flexibility required to meet all needs. You may not be able to meet all needs within one presentation, but when you take questions, be conscious of the thinking pattern of the questioner which you can spot through the tell-tale signs – and answer the questions in their style.

How you are viewed by others

You will have a stronger thinking preference and will find it more comfortable to use your stronger preference. You have varying strengths of preference. You are not one or the other. You have developed this practice since birth and will have at least twenty years of serious practice. And if you have a strong preference it's likely that you will be excellent at using it.

How you are perceived by another individual and how you see others depends on where you are on the continuum, of say, Big Picture–Detail. Let's say you are quite strongly big picture. You may describe A as detail and A will describe you as big picture. B is quite close to you but less big picture. You will still describe them as detail because that's how they appear to you. B will describe you as big picture because you are more big picture than him. B may describe A as very detailed and have more difficulty connecting with him than B does with you.

Externally referenced and internally referenced

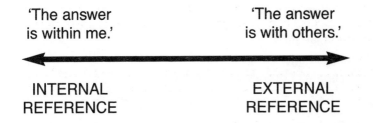

'The answer is within me.'   'The answer is with others.'

INTERNAL REFERENCE   EXTERNAL REFERENCE

figure 14 the internal–external reference continuum

This thinking pattern concerns how you judge and decide if something is good or not. The external/internal refers to where you locate your judgement – and how you use it as a reference. Externally referenced people evaluate on the basis of what others think. In contrast, internally referenced people make the decision based on what they think. Churchill was extremely self-referenced as shown in his stance on opposition to Nazi Germany before the Second World War. He knew he was right though few agreed with him at that time. There is a downside to Churchill's strong self-referenced thinking pattern. When things were going badly in Gallipoli during the First World War, he did not seek advice from others because he felt he was right. As a consequence thousands of British and Australian troops were lost.

Margaret Thatcher was strongly internally referenced. When the countries in the Commonwealth were negotiating whether to impose sanctions on South Africa during its Apartheid period, the vote was 49 to one in favour of sanctions. The one vote was cast by the United Kingdom, and significantly by Margaret Thatcher. When the vote was announced, Thatcher declared, 'I feel sorry for the other forty-nine'.

Internally referenced

Judy: 'I am not impressed by the plans. The merger hasn't been successful in my view, and creating large R&D groups doesn't work.'

Internally referenced thinkers:
- Use their own feelings to know if they have done a good job
- No amount of praise from others will convince them if they believe they have not met their own target
- Rely on their own views to make decisions
- Are convinced when you appeal to things they already know through their own experiences

Tell-tale signs:
- They tell us firmly when they decide
- They say – 'I decide', 'I just know'. Feedback from others doesn't tell them when they have done a good job
- They resist when someone else attempts to tell them what's happening

How to communicate with internally referenced thinkers:
- Ask them what they think. Avoid telling them what others feel about the situation
- Help them to identify their own thinking
- Support an alternative, but say 'that only you will know how to complete this task'. This keeps the notion of choice within themselves and thus they are more likely to consider your proposal as it remains in their control
- To convince Judy, Elaine would have to provide Judy with the information she needs to make up her own mind, and could within the presentation ask Judy and others – 'you can ask yourself if you have enough information to make your own mind up', which will move them towards a decision

Externally referenced

Susan: 'They make all these grand claims – but where's the industry benchmark reports that show our products are 'second to none'?'

Externally referenced thinkers:
- Require direction from others' and rely on others' views and opinions
- Draw conclusions based on others' views
- Let others make decisions on how to do it
- Conform to others' beliefs
- Constantly want to know what others think

Tell-tale signs:
- Ask for lots of feedback on how well things went
- Says 'the facts speak for themselves', 'they told me this was a good idea', 'this is the way it is'
- May describe incoming external information as a decision

How to communicate with externally referenced thinkers:
- Emphasize what other people think, especially authority figures
- Give lots of external data such as statistics
- Emphasize often 'other people think'
- To convince Susan, Elaine would need to offer industry evidence of benchmarking against world class practice

Options and procedures thinkers

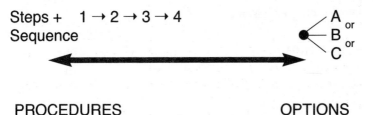

figure 15 the options–procedures thinkers continuum

Options thinkers

Simone: 'The statement is OK but seems quite restrictive. Yes it's good to provide unmatched support but there are lots of ways of providing support that aren't mentioned, and certainly we can offer products other than network systems.'

Option thinkers:
- Are excited by possibilities, what might be, desire to learn and like to expand options
- Are curious about the unknown and what may develop
- Are good at developing new procedures and once implemented will consider changing them even though they may be working well

Tell-tale signs:

- Lots of words such as 'choose', 'hope', and 'wish'
- Talk about expanding options and exploration of the unknown
- Use action-oriented verbs – 'I will complete this task and get results'
- Let's do something different this time

How to communicate with options thinkers:

- Provide them with choices in how to implement. Asking them to follow a procedure will cause them difficulty
- Emphasize choices in task completion
- Use words such as 'possibilities', 'choices', 'new ways', 'and alternatives'

Simone, the options thinker, would find Elaine's statement appealing: 'The new merger provides us with many alternatives in how we carry forward the business. Each business unit will be able to create their own world in whatever way they choose to live out our new vision.'

Procedures

Michael: 'The difficulty with that presentation is that it's not clear how we are to proceed. There were too many loose ends.'

Procedures thinkers:

- Are motivated by 'need', 'obligation' and necessity. Procedures thinkers are motivated to do something because they must, rather than wanting to do it
- When they want to do something, they want to know the 'right' way to do it
- Have a tendency to accept what comes rather than seek that which is possible
- Stay with what is known and secure

Tell-tale signs:

- Use words such as 'have to', 'must', 'ought to', 'should', 'always'
- Don't talk about options. Procedures thinkers give the impression that they have to or are obliged to do things and that there isn't a choice. Choice and change may unsettle them
- They like to know in advance what will happen and then stick to it

How to communicate with procedures thinkers:

- Emphasize the procedures – lay them out step by step, and keep them informed of the steps
- Tell them it's always been done this way when helping them to understand. Even when you are asked for different ways, indicate (as there is in some organizations) there is a procedure for being creative
- Use words such as 'procedure', 'proven ways', 'correct way', 'known way', 'and appropriate'

Michael will be attracted to Elaine's statement, 'There are choices available for each business unit but we have a proven and successful procedure for choosing the correct way. Each business unit will use the Edward de Bono "thinking hats" procedure to generate their ideas for their business plans.'

Similarity and difference

Before reading on look at the shapes in Figure 16 and describe the relationship between them. How you describe the relationship gives evidence of your preferred patterns.

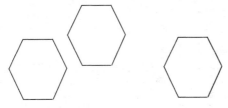

What do you see?

figure 16 the similarity and difference relationship

Similarity

Dorothy: 'The vision is so new and different. It makes me feel uncomfortable as does working with these new people from Technica.'

If you noticed the shapes were similar and nothing else you have a preference for similarity.

Similarity thinkers:

- Tend to look for what's there as opposed to what's missing and match what you are saying with what they already know
- Generalize too quickly based on a few examples especially when they are alike: 'Ah, that's the same problem, we had a similar problem with two other suppliers'

Tell-tale signs:

- They use words such as 'same', 'similar', 'in common', 'maintains', 'keep the same'
- They will tell you how a set of objects or situations are similar

How to communicate with similarity thinkers:

- Emphasize areas of mutual agreement
- Discuss familiarity with current and previous situations
- Focus on mutual objectives
- Use words such as 'similar', 'in common', 'maintain', 'keep the same'

You need to emphasize the similarity with the past, and help Dorothy to focus on what is the same: 'Our focus is as it has always been. Our common themes have been: customer service and responses to customers. We will maintain our standards, and then gradually increase them, as we have in the past.'

Difference

Maire: 'There's nothing new in the initiative. It's not worthwhile.'

If you looked at the hexagons diagram and noticed one was higher, lower, left, right, you are likely to run differences. People who use this pattern notice what is different – and often disagree with your view immediately.

Difference thinkers:

- Tend to sort for what's missing
- Will mismatch as a way to understanding. They naturally make the opposite point so they can understand. You may interpret this response as persistent and unnecessary objecting. You may even say they are 'awkward', 'bloody-minded', or 'twisted'. Remember *behaviour is not identity* – they are using their preferred pattern – mismatching!
- Will notice how things don't fit together

Tell-tale signs:

- Use phrases like 'day and night', 'no relationship', 'no comparison'
- You will hear the phrases 'yes, but', 'no, but' a lot
- Discuss how 'things have changed'; 'I am completely different'
- They use words such as 'new', 'changed', 'radical' and 'revolutionary'

How to communicate with differences:

- Emphasize the differences
- Present ideas in the frame of being very different
- Use their 'tell-tale' words

Maire would be comfortable with a response: 'While our vision remains the same as it was in Technica and Worldlink [we have just said this to appeal to the Similarity thinkers] there is much that is more radical thinking; we will redesign our customer care to be even more customer focused ...'

Using both similarities and difference

Each program has been drawn on a continuum. Thus our preferred position can range from very strong preference for similarities, to very strong preference for difference. In the middle it is likely that we use both. In his book *Hiring, Managing, Selling for Peak Performances*, Roger Bailey presents research that shows we use both these preferences in a particular pattern.

When you examined the shapes in Figure 16, you may have noticed similarities in shape, then some differences. You have seen three identical hexagons, and then thought one is to the left, one is higher, one further apart. People who run this pattern will tell you how things are the same or similar with secondary emphasis on the different – they will use phrases like:

- 'It's almost the same basically – but it will work better.'
- 'The mission statement is more or less the same – with a gradual improvement in customer care.'

This pattern of similarity is thought to be run by 55–65 per cent of the population who don't mind some change, but with a limit!

Difference with some similarity is run by 20–25 per cent of the population. People who run this pattern spotted differences in the shapes, and then some exceptions that are similarities. They will use phrases such as:

- 'Most things round here have changed, though I still have the same role.'
- 'The new strategy will change everything here except we will still focus our value for money initiative!'

People who run difference consistently are called *mismatchers*. If you say something is black, their immediate response will be 'it could be white'. McNish, the carpenter with Shackleton on *Endurance*, was a *mismatcher*. When Shackleton told him something was 'impossible' he said 'No, it's not. I can do it.' The out-and-out difference thinkers, the mismatchers, are 5–10 per cent of the population. Those people who run mismatch really are a stretch to work with. They suggest the opposite to almost all suggestions. If you want to influence them, you need to support the opposite of what your desired behaviour is. If you want them to join a team, you say 'you wouldn't want to join that team. It's not your kind of project!' The response may be 'No I would, and it is'.

Be careful in trying this pattern of mismatching to agreement. Check it out first with less significant behaviour – like a choice of sandwich, drink etc. – and remember even mismatchers have some habits that are fixed.

The remaining 5–10 per cent sort for similarity and difference equally. They will say 'the more things change, the more they will stay the same'.

Moving away from–Moving towards

AWAY FROM

TOWARDS

figure 17 the moving away from–moving towards continuum

Moving away

Joshua: 'It's another crazy push forwards. I bet they haven't thought of how we'll increase the sales force to cope with the new business, or how we are going to produce all the new products, let alone the changes that will be required in my department. At least they have acknowledged our history in network systems, and 12 years' experience in customer support. Nonetheless this change is dangerous.'

Away from thinkers:
- Move away from problems they don't want or like
- Often have trouble defining what they *do* want and can have difficulty with goals
- Focus on negative consequences and may be overly distracted by them

Tell-tale signs:
- They talk about what they don't want, and what they don't want to happen
- They tell you what they will 'avoid', 'stay away from' and 'get out of'

How to communicate with away from thinkers:
- Find out what they don't want, and empathize that you can help them avoid what they don't want
- Anticipate problems, and reassure them the problem can be solved
- Be patient with their potential inability to tell you what they want

Joshua would be reassured by the response: 'I understand there are issues with merging departments and providing the best customer support. We will build on what we have done successfully before, use the experience we have in dealing with change, and plan to provide the resources to support the inevitable problems of change.'

Moving towards

Ali was pleased with Elaine's statement. He could envisage the successful merger and what it would contribute to the vision.

People who move towards:
- Move towards what they want
- Often have difficulty in recognizing what should be avoided

- Often minimize negative consequences, or are even oblivious to what is not working as they work in pursuit of their goal.

The analysis of many man-made disasters points to the disastrous consequences of 'moving towards' thinking. One theory is that the explosion at the Chernobyl Nuclear Plant in the Ukraine was caused by scientists attempting to prove the safety qualities of the plant and who pushed equipment to the limit and ignored the warning signs.

Tell-tale signs:
- They talk about what they want
- They talk about people and things they want to include
- They use words like 'attain', 'gain', 'accomplish' 'obtain', 'achieve'

Communicating with towards people
- Focus on the stated goals and what they want to achieve
- Emphasize that what you are doing will help them to get what they want

It is likely that you will run both patterns with a primary motivation and a secondary follow up. You may be motivated towards, and check on what can go wrong, or you may consider first what you wish to avoid, and then move towards what you wish to achieve.

Entrepreneurs, both inside and outside an organization, tend to be *towards*. They go for goals and often don't fully consider the downside. Lawyers and safety experts use mostly *away from* patterns, helping you avoid unpleasant consequences. The clash between the patterns can be interesting – 'I just want to close this deal' (the towards person), 'but what if A happens, and B ... and Z' (the away from person) – and as we need to remind ourselves, both approaches are just different thinking patterns that result in different behaviours.

More patterns of thinking

You have considered the five key thinking patterns that you will have to be aware of in your effective communications with others. When you begin to be more conscious of those patterns you will discover many more.

Hall and Bodenhamer, in *Figuring Out People*, present 51 patterns of thinking. Their view is that the patterns fit into four categories:

- Ways of thinking and processing information
- Methods of choosing and being
- Responding to others
- Identifying of self

Other main patterns that will be spotted in others are shown by categories with the five patterns discussed already shown in italics.

- **Ways of thinking:**
  Detail/big picture
  Similarity/difference
  Senses – Visual Auditory Kinesthetic (from Chapter 6)

- **Methods of choosing:**
  Associated/disassociated (from Chapter 4)
  Away from/towards
  Options/procedures
  Internal/external
  Proactive/reactive – whether you 'jump in' or wait to see what will happen

- **Responding to others:**
  Things/people – your focus of interest is on what are the things or how you respond to people
  Independent/team player/manager – where you focus your attentions and interest in the work situation.

- **Identity of self**
  Past/present/future – which time period do you concern yourself with – past, present, future?
  Closure/openness – coming to conclusion quickly or keeping options open

---

EXERCISE: Analysis of self

Without an understanding of your own thinking patterns, you may well delete important data about people. You may be comfortable with the people with whom you share patterns, and find opposites too difficult to work with. The behavioural indicators are based on Eric Robbie's work as described in *Figuring Out People*. Tick the box closest to the description of yourself.

	Big picture		**Detail**	
If you are asked to work on a big project do you first	need to know about the overall goal, purpose?	☐ *or*	need a precise and organized structure for the project?	☐

	Big picture		**Detail**	
When describing a project do you use your hands	in big gestures	☐ or	in small detailed movements?	☐

	Internal		**External**	
When you have completed a project do you	know whether it's good or bad?	☐ or	ask others about its value?	☐
When you are deciding on the value of something, do you	use your self-talk to give an answer?	☐ or	look outside for others to talk to?	☐

	Options		**Procedures**	
When you are asked your views on development activities for you, do you first think of	lots of alternative approaches?	☐ or	the systematic process that is required to get your development needs identified?	☐
When you are considering how to tackle a problem do your hands	count off the alternatives available on your fingers?	☐ or	gesture in space as if sequencing them?	☐

	Similarity		**Difference**	
When you are buying a new product do you first	compare it to other products and look for sameness?	☐ or	identify what are the unique and different features?	☐
When thinking of choosing a new product, do your hands	gesture together and come towards each other?	☐ or	gesture apart at odd angles?	☐

	Moving away		**Towards**	
When you consider what you want in a job, do you first think of	things you don't want – like excessive travel, hours, or paperwork?	☐ or	the challenge, stretching, points within the role?	☐
When you consider what you want from a project, during a meeting, does your head	lean more back?	☐ or	move forwards and back?	☐

Now consider the five patterns you have chosen. How well do they describe you? Your preference may range from very strong to no strong preference.

How you can change your patterns of thinking

The focus of this chapter is about communicating with others and as you read about the patterns of thinking you may have identified patterns you use that are not useful. For example, you may have recognized that in your desire to reach goals (the *towards* pattern) you have ignored some key issues that might stop you (the *away froms*). In working with the Managing Director of a fast-growing company and discussing yet more acquisitions, the authors asked him, 'What happens if you become seriously ill?' The response was 'I won't and we'll still get there.' Eventually key person insurance was bought to cover the potential illness in order to keep the business going if something happened to him, i.e. an away from. If he ran 'away from' it would have been purchased years ago – as also would the pension, and other life assurance products.

Alternatively you may be able to articulate well what you didn't want – but not what you do. It can be said of political parties in opposition that often they know what they don't want (i.e. the ruling party's policy) but they don't know what they do want.

EXERCISE: Change your pattern of thinking

Your pattern of thinking can be stretched and adjusted. Since the patterns inform the brain about what to sort and delete, if, for example, you move *towards* you delete or pay less attention to what you move away from, and if you move *away from* you delete or pay less attention to what you move towards. If you direct your conscious thoughts to the deleted part you can access more resource and choice in your behaviour. The stages are:

1 Identify the pattern that currently does not serve you well and undermines your effectiveness.

2 Describe the thinking pattern you wish to use more readily. Read over the text above and indicate why, where, and when you wish to use it.

3 Try it out in your head. Say the words that will be unfamiliar, think the pattern that is different. If you know someone who runs the pattern you would like, put yourself in that second position you discussed in Chapter 6 – and see, feel, and hear what they would do.

4 Check that you really want to change the pattern in the context you are thinking of. You have learned it well over the years, and it has had a positive intention for you. Decide if the new behaviour is how you want to be. How will the new behaviour, and use of a different pattern, affect you and others around you?

5 If you have satisfactory answers to the above, 'install' the new pattern. Give yourself permission to use it. You are, after all, *in charge of your own brain*! You may find that your self-talk will point out a difficulty. If you decided to use towards, a voice from your past, parent/professional adviser, might say, 'Be careful, if you don't think about what might go wrong you'll lose everything – so don't do it.' Listen to these concerns and answer them. Say to the voice, 'I will be careful, I will consider all the stages, and the loss is of such a value – so I can't lose everything.'

6 Think of how the pattern will work in the future – and use it until it becomes comfortable.

And you have permission to change back!

Learning for leadership success

In this chapter you have explored five thinking patterns and how you can alter your message to influence people with different positions, namely:

• Big picture–detail
• Externally referenced–internally referenced
• Options–procedures
• Similarity–difference
• Moving away from–moving towards

And as you begin to be aware of patterns you will notice many others, possibly beyond the 51 that Bodenhamer and Hall have identified.

08

communicating powerfully

In this chapter you will learn:
- how to use *precision language* to gain a richer understanding of others' *maps*
- *artfully vague language* to help others to create rich and compelling meaning in what you say
- to consider the three words that stop others from performing – '*can't*', '*try*', and '*but*'

'If you can dream it, you can do it.'
Walt Disney

'Everything should be made as simple as possible, but not simpler.'
Albert Einstein

Introduction

In this chapter we will look at two techniques of communication that will give you the choices in how you powerfully influence others. These techniques focus on the use of language.

As a leader you will want to powerfully communicate with your followers. You want to be able to determine precisely what a person means by the words he or she uses. The use of language can give your follower a different way of thinking about something that gives it another meaning for them – and that other meaning can give them choices. In doing so you get the more precise view of their 'map'. *Precision questioning* gives you these skills. At other times you can powerfully communicate by using artfully vague language such that the follower can access thoughts and resources that may be hidden. With more resources they can be more flexible in their actions. How you help followers to connect with these resources is the role of *artfully vague language* and the words you use can make people feel powerless to act. We suggest that you cease to use the three words that disempower – *can't, try, but.*

EXERCISE

You will need to involve two or three others in this exercise. Write down five words that mean entertainment to you. Ask two other people to complete the same task. Now compare the lists.

Analysis

You may find some commonality and much difference. When we completed this exercise with our colleagues, Sean stated entertainment to be 'fun, company, enjoyment, music and frivolity'. Anne said it was 'TV, cinema, theatre, musicals and videos'. In this instance Anne chose to describe the *how* of entertainment rather than the *what*. A third colleague, Mavis, had 'fun, conversation, dining out and skiing' on her list, a mixture of what and how. We asked her 'what specifically do you mean by

---

fun?' She said 'going shopping with my girlfriends'. Sean, when asked 'what is fun?' said 'playing golf with my colleagues'. Note the difference. Yet everyone knows what fun is! If you have not completed the exercise it will make sense that we have different meanings for words and the meaning is only about an intellectual level. Remember the time you said to your partner, 'let's have an entertaining weekend' – and they designed the weekend from hell – for you! So there is no commonality on the meaning of entertainment. If you haven't done the exercise, please do it now.

The background to precision language

In their book, *Precision: A New Approach to Communication*, Michael McMaster and John Grinder comment: 'The same businessman who accepts as adequate – "increasing productivity in the next 3 months" would fire an assistant who told him he had a business appointment late Friday afternoon, somewhere in LA.'

You are going to consider twelve questioning patterns that will allow you to get to the meaning of a communication with a person. To help you understand the questioning process it is useful to understand the difference between the *surface* and *deep structure of language*.

Surface structure is represented by the words or sentences that you speak. Deep structure is the *internal representation*, the experience of what you seek to communicate. Deep structure is what you really want to say but it is not conscious. If you used deep structure to communicate you would become very long winded – so what you do is *delete*, *distort* and *generalize*, as discussed in the Leadership Communication Model in Chapter 6. The message becomes the shorter but less precise message at surface level.

Using *precision language* you seek to unravel the *generalizations*, *deletions* and *distortions* that others use and get to their deep structure, to their 'map' of the world. If you do this you can begin to communicate within their map. Otherwise you may speak at cross-purposes, with subsequent confusion.

Case study: generalization–deletion–distortion

Jim was presenting on the notion of keeping close to the customer and providing world-class service – and in doing so, treating each of the customers as you would treat a member of your own family. He noticed that one of the managers, Sam, listened, then said out loud – 'Yuk, what a stupid idea'. Jim's first thought was that the manager was unreceptive to the message. His second thought was that he had just learned about the Leadership Communication Model and also the notion of how you distort, delete and generalize such that our surface message isn't our deep one. So rather than snap at Sam for being rude he thought 'what could have happened in Sam's mind?'

Sam had a specific thought when he heard the phrase 'treat them like your family'. His thought was 'I remember when Sheila, my sister-in-law, was screaming like a witch at me and I screamed back. That's not what I wanted to do.'

The first stage is to move away from the specific thought to the *generalization* that all family members yell at you like witches. Sam *distorted* the thought to 'customers as family members yelling at you like witches', so that thought is *deleted* such that customers become witches and he says 'yuk, what a stupid idea'. The stupid idea is not related to Sam's notion that 'we treat customers as family' but to his own internal representation. And going back to the Leadership Communication Model, if Jim responds to Sam's stimulus by saying 'how dare you say I'm stupid …?' you begin to see the dangers of acting on imprecise communication at the surface level.

Case study: deep structure level

A company asked for a review of their communications strategy. They were committed to open and direct communication. The report from the consultants contained quotations from the staff members that appeared to raise more questions than answers. The Director of Communications of this company, Asif, wanted to get finer detail in order to plan the necessary changes. He wanted to get the level of information required at a deep structure level. The phrases that he wanted to dig deeper into were:

'They don't listen to me in this organization.'
'I feel as if I am being manipulated.'
'Communication is better in the sales department.'

'My supervisor handled the communication meeting badly.'

'It's clear that we need to improve how we present our message.'

'What is required is more honesty and respect in our communication.'

'I can't make sense of what is being said.'

'We must provide an in-company newsletter. Everyone issues an in-company newsletter.'

'I know that all the managers are worried about communication.'

'Communication will never work here, until senior managers are more open.'

'When we get the IT system in place, we will be able to improve communication.'

'Because the senior managers won't talk directly to us, they don't want to tell us what's happening.'

The Director of Communication knew who had made each statement, and chose to go back to interview each person again in order to be able to get to the deeper meaning of the message.

How to use precision language

To take you through how to get deeper meaning from surface statements each phrase from the above case study will be discussed and you will be shown how to use precision language to move from *surface* to *deep structure*. Twelve categories of precision question are discussed.

Unspecified nouns

'**They** don't listen to me in this organization.'

In this case Asif doesn't know who 'they' are. It could be co-workers, supervisors, managers or any other group. Unspecified nouns are clarified by using the question, '*Who (or what) specifically?*'

Unspecified verbs

'I feel as if I am being **manipulated**.'

The verb 'manipulate' is vague and non-specific. Manipulate describes an action or process but so much information is deleted that you cannot have a clear representation of the meaning of the action. Was it that the person behaved against their will, or was stopped from doing something, or just felt bad? If you need more detail on the manipulation you need to ask *'How specifically did … ?'*

Comparison

'Communication is **better** in the sales department.'

'My supervisors handled our communication meeting **badly**.'

In the first statement communication is being compared with other departments through the use of 'better'. But you need to know better than what. Better than it was before? Better than the manufacturing or administration department? When you use 'best', 'better', 'worse', or 'worst' you are making a comparison. You can only make a comparison when you know compared to what.

In the second statement the judgement is made that the supervisor handles communication meetings 'badly'. 'Badly' compared to what? How the person who made the statement would have done it? How his manager would have handled it? How a 'superman' communicator would have handled it?

Often the deleted part of the comparison is unrealistic. If someone had said to you 'You handled that presentation badly' and had deleted the unsaid comparison (compared with a brilliant presenter), you are left with a feeling of inadequacy. And you may then believe there is nothing you can do about improving your presentation skills.

If you wish to clarify a comparison you ask, *'Compared with what, whom …?'*

Judgement

'**It's clear** that we need to improve how we present our message.'

This statement raises the question 'clear to whom?' The management team, the individual, the whole company? And on what grounds is it clear? Where is the evidence that makes it clear? Do we have customer feedback, a survey completed, or is it one person's view?' To clarify the judgements you need to ask: *'Who is making the judgement, and what evidence do they have for making it?'*

Actions into nouns

'What is required is more **honesty** and **respect** in our **communication**.'

You have already considered one verb turned into a noun when you were asked to get others' views on the meaning of entertainment. Entertainment is what happens to an individual or a group. It involves action. It is not a static process.

In the statement above there are three verbs turned into nouns – honesty, respect and communication. Each needs to be explored to recover the process and action. To discover more meaning you need to ask *'How would you know they were honest?'*. You need to ask *'Who's not communicating?'*, *'How would you like to communicate?'*, *'How should others communicate?'* With 'respect' you need to ask, *'Who is respecting whom and how are they doing it?'*

Turning actions into nouns can often make the recipient helpless and lack choices. When we were coaching a senior manager, he claimed that he 'had high levels of stress'. 'High levels of stress' can be seen as a fixed phenomenon over which the manager has no control: it happens to him. If we take the 'noun' and ask what actions are causing it, you would ask him 'How are you stressing yourself?' his response to this was 'I'm working too long hours: this project is very complex.' He gave himself more choice in what to do. He began to think about how he could reduce the hours, to get other people involved and to break the project down into simpler stages. And more importantly he now felt in control of what was happening to him. He had moved from *effect*, from having high levels of stress, to *cause*, he stresses himself and thus in charge of his own destiny. It may be that by turning actions into nouns you create the most misleading language pattern.

To clarify meaning you need to ask the person to turn the noun back into action by asking, for example, *'Who is communicating about what and how are they doing it?'*

Language of possibility

'I **can't** make sense of what is being said.'

The person who made this statement has defined in their map of the world, that they can't (ever) make sense of the statements. If they remain of this viewpoint they will continue not to be able to make sense of it. Most people can, if they want to make the effort, make sense of something. It may be that the person is choosing not to make sense – for many reasons that are contained in their experience, memories, belief and values. The 'I can't' becomes an absolute state, not amenable to change.

The language of possibility contains words such as: can/can't; possible/impossible; will/won't, and may/may not. The questions that get clarification are: *'What stops you from ...?'*, *'What would happen if you did ...?'*

Language of necessity

'We **must** provide an in-company newsletter.'

Implied in this statement is a rule of conduct that is not explicit. You have no idea for the basis for the rule. If you take action and implement the newsletter you may miss other opportunities for reaching the implied goal, better communications. The use of 'must' and 'should' when you talk to someone often implies failure in the other person. A feeling of guilt that they should be able to do the task is instilled.

Clarification on 'must/must not', 'should/shouldn't', 'have to', 'need to', 'and it is necessary to' is achieved by asking: *'What would happen if you did/didn't ...?'*, *'Or?'*

Generalization

'**Everyone** issues an in-company newsletter.'

Generalization is a very common form of imprecise language. A limited experience is taken to apply to an entire category. The person who said this has experience of companies that have newsletters and has generalized to all companies. Generalizations are limiting as they preclude exceptions. Recognition of the exceptions allows us to be more realistic. Generalizations often include *unspecified verbs* (issues) and *unspecified nouns* (in-company newsletter).

You can spot generalizations by the words 'every', 'all', 'never', 'no one'. Sometimes the generalization is implied as in 'email messages are the key to effective communication'. The person who states this has not been faced with, or does not remember, the 200 new mail messages that have arrived in the morning – many of which are no use. Challenges to generalizations that flush out the exceptions are to bounce back the generalization as a challenging question: *'All ...?'*, *'Never ...?'* and *'Has there ever been a time when ...?'*

Mind reading

'**I know** all the managers are worried about communication.'

This statement appears to be a significant endorsement of the need for the investment in the new communications system. The manager may have thought about communication and she may well be worried – she is assuming, without any evidence, that others share her concerns. If this manager was talking to other managers and said 'I know you all are worried about communication', she may set up a self-fulfilling cycle where they begin to believe they should be worried, and begin to be! Challenge to the mind-reader is to ask: '*How exactly do you know ...?*'

Cause and effect

'Communications will never work here, **until** senior managers **are more open.**'

In this statement the problem is 'communications' and has been shifted to the senior managers. If they are more open then communication will work better. This form of distortion puts the individual who stated this at the control of senior managers. It may be true that senior managers need to be more open – and there are also actions that this manager could take to improve communications. Challenges to cause and effect are: '*How specifically does ... cause ...?*'

Presuppositions

'When we get the IT system in place, we will be able to improve communication.'

This statement incorporates previous beliefs and *expectations* that presuppose 'if the IT system is in place' communication will be improved. It may be necessary to challenge this basic assumption as it limits choice. Communication can be improved by other means – the initial challenge to the *presupposition* is '*What makes you believe that ...?*'

Complex relationship

'Because the senior managers won't talk directly to us, they don't want to tell us what is happening.'

There is some mind reading in this statement on the links between the two parts of the statements. Senior managers may wish to cascade communication down through the organization and do not choose to do so, as they wish the immediate manager to undertake the task. There is no evidence that because 'senior managers don't talk directly to us' that 'they don't want to tell us what is happening'.

The question to find out more about the complex relationship in the person's map is 'How does x mean y?'

Conclusion

You have considered twelve patterns that allow us to probe into the deep structure of someone's map to get a richer and fuller understanding of their world. In doing so you explore further the three map-making processes of generalization, deletion and distortion. You can also use the same questioning on your own self-talk. The next time you say 'I can't', (a language of possibility) ask yourself 'What's stopping me?'

EXERCISE

In reality a sentence may often contain more than one example of imprecise language. Identify the pattern within this sentence and compare to the given correct answer.

'Why don't the incompetent directors stop trying to communicate with me? It always just annoys me. I know I should remain calmer but I can't.'

Answer

This sentence contains *mind reading* and *presuppositions* (the directors are trying to annoy me), *cause and effect* (communication annoys me), *generalization* (always), *judgement* (incompetent), *comparison* (calmer), *language of possibility* (can't), *language of necessity* (should), *unspecified verbs* (trying), *actions into nouns* (calm), and *unspecified nouns* (IT, directors).

The benefits of precision questioning

Exploring the deep structure of meaning using precision language is very powerful as it:

- Allows you to gather the high quality data so you understand what people mean. So you get into their *map* rather than assuming meaning. You avoid your frustrating cry (inwards or stated) of 'But I thought you meant …'. Note that there are no 'why' questions – we often use the thought that 'why implies blame'. Blame is not the purpose, but clarity of understanding is, thus avoid 'why'.

Ask yourself the question 'Why did I not understand the ... last section on complex relationships?' A small voice may say 'you stupid person'. Compare your feeling to that from 'What did I not understand from the last section on complex relationships?' You will feel that it is simply something you didn't understand.

- Provides clarity of meaning so you know exactly what the other person means.
- Gives you choices: generalization, actions with nouns, and presuppositions all set limits – and the limits exist in the word, not in the world. If you believe 'no one can achieve that' (a generalization), the words provide a limit to your actions. What if Roger Bannister had believed that 'no one could run a four-minute mile?

In the sentence in the exercise above, you were faced with twelve examples of imprecise language in only two sentences. But in leadership situations you may not have the time to analyse as you did above. Joseph O'Connor and John Seymour in *Introducing Neuro-Linguistic Programming*, suggest that if you explore the patterns in the following order you gain most clarity for your effort. Group 1 gains the most clarity.

1 Mindreading, presupposition and cause and effect. That the 'directors try to annoy me' and 'communication annoys me' is at the heart of the complaint – if you ask 'How exactly do you know ...' (the precision question for mind reading), the 'problem' may become, 'Well, actually they are trying to tell me'. These three patterns fuel all the other patterns.

2 Unspecified verbs, unspecified nouns, performer, comparisons, language of possibility and necessity. That the directors are 'incompetent' (judgement), and 'should' (the language of necessity) are less critical in getting to the meaning compared with the biggest issue of 'How exactly do you know'. If there is no evidence that the 'directors are trying to annoy', there is no basis for concern about 'shoulds' and 'judgements'.

3 Actions in nouns, unspecified nouns, unspecified verbs. These are the least important as you explore very fine meaning. 'What specifically do you mean by director?' is of limited impact compared with the mindread, that 'the director is trying to annoy me'. Challenging the mindread is more powerful than challenging 'the who' is trying to annoy you.

From experience we find that it is often the less powerful precision questions that are overused. At leadership training we often hear over the dinner table, 'What specifically do you mean by wine, port ... etc.'. Possibly amusing at first, it can begin to irritate the speaker as the imprecision in every sentence is exposed, and the flow of communication is interrupted. You move quickly towards a 'stop doing that'. You may move towards precision but with the critical potential loss of *rapport*. So be cautious of overusing precision questions and remember that if you break *rapport*, you will not get the information you want in order to influence.

EXERCISE

You have considered twelve precision patterns and the precision questions that provide more in-depth data. The table below shows the pattern in summary.

Pattern	Precision question
Unspecified noun	Who (or what) specifically?
Unspecified verbs	How specifically did?
Comparison	Compared with what, when?
Performer	Who is making the judgement?
Actions into nouns	Who is ... and how are they doing it?
Language of possibility	What stops you?
Language of necessity	What would happen if you didn't do that?
Generalization	Everyone?
Mind reading	How exactly do you know?
Cause and effect	How specifically does 'this' cause 'that'?
Complex relationship	How does 'this' mean 'that'?
Presupposition	What makes you believe?

Now photocopy the table, and put it into your pocket, organizer, or have a copy available at meetings. Pick one pattern for each of the next twelve days and listen for its use. If useful, challenge the pattern. You will find that you will soon have the model in your unconscious and it is a resource that is available to use. Be cautious of misuse and losing rapport.

Enjoy the magic of precision questioning.

'Artfully vague' language to create meaning

'That's a great deal to make one word mean,' Alice said in a thoughtful tone.
'When I make a word do a lot of work like that,' said Humpty Dumpty, 'I always pay extra.'

Lewis Carroll, *Alice through the Looking Glass*

Precision language allows you to get to the deeper meaning that people have in their heads. Now you can learn 'artfully vague' language, to allow followers to create their own 'new world' to which they wish to belong. In doing so you may win their hearts and minds because you will engage their emotions and increase rapport with them.

With artfully vague language you deliberately choose to use unspecified verbs and nouns that allow the listener to make their own interpretation in their 'world' to positively create their own generalizations, distortion and deletion. This technique is the opposite of precision questioning which is useful to drill down to the meaning at a deeper level. An inspirational speech will use 'artfully vague' language to allow the individual to create meaning. For example in his inaugural speech in 1963, John F. Kennedy stated: *'And so, my fellow Americans ask not what your country can do for you, ask what you can do for your country.'* The follower can choose what they wish to 'do', and there is ambiguity in what is 'your country' and much else in this one phrase.

You will probably recognize this skilful use of language in many modern advertising slogans. The model for the artfully vague language patterns was Milton Erickson who was an expert creator of trance conditions that allowed, in his case, clients to access their internal resources. The patterns he used are often referred to as the Milton Model. A key part of his technique was first to build *rapport* with clients so they would be open to his suggestions of new resources.

This technique can be applied in your leadership. When you use artfully vague language, the follower must fill in the details and actively search for the meaning of what is heard from *their own experience*, and in doing so, allow you to connect with their experience. In the example below, Sian is making a presentation to a mixed audience with different values, beliefs, and views and she wishes to appeal to all. The following description shows how Sian has skilfully used the technique of *artfully vague language*. You will also see that she uses the influencing technique of match–pace–lead:

Match with the Yes set

Create the conditions in which the followers are saying 'yes, yes, yes', which creates a positive direction with them. This is a common part of influencing where you want to get the follower to say 'yes'. As Sian says:

'Hi, I'm Sian O'Hara. We are here today [*yes*] after the planning work that has gone on in the last months [*yes*]. Some of you will want to have the broad picture and some the final detail [the choice of two means mismatchers (discussed in Chapter 7) will have to say *yes* to one!] This session is to meet your needs!'

Pace

Pacing is critical to build rapport so the audience is receptive to the message. It is likely that the rapport will come from an area outside the work environment and come from common human experience that all can relate to, such as raising a family, going to school, and choosing a group such as accountants or lawyers who have different views. Sian continues:

'The creation of the marketing plan has been like raising a child, and you will recognize the stages in the process as either a parent or child or both. The early years are full of wonderment and first learning, then we get to school and rules are imposed (in our case by the accountants rather than the teachers), and then we go through adolescence – a bit uncertain – and then to maturity where we know we can do it!'

Lead

In this stage you introduce in an artfully vague way the reverse of the patterns from precision language. Doing this allows listeners to value their experience, and a sense of what is happening and to lead them towards a positive and exciting internal representation. Sian is moving them forward, allowing her followers to create a world that she wants them to join. Read the speech in a piece and then see how the language is artfully vague.

'I know that you are curious and that means you will learn that much better about our success last year. It's a good thing to consider first what happened last year and to base the plan on this experience. We will be able to go forward to greater achievements next year. We must be focused on next year, so what is the plan all about?'

Language	Interpretation
'I know that you are curious …	*Mindread* that embeds the command that individuals are curious.
… and that means you will learn …	*Complex relationship* that implies being curious means that you will learn.
… that much better about our success last year.'	*Comparison* – better than whatever comparison People choose, but still learn better.
'It's a good thing to consider first what happened last year …	*Judgement* – who says, and the command is that it is a good thing.
… and to base the plan on this experience.'	*Complex relationship* again – another command that plans should be based on last year.
'We will be able to go forward to greater achievements next year.'	*Comparison and action in noun* – each person can select their own achievement – and make it greater.
'We must …	*Language of necessity* – really meaning the organization states that
… be focused on next year …'	*Unspecified verb* – each focus in their own way.

The key to the creation of artfully vague language is to utilize as opposites all those patterns that you analysed in precision questioning. You do not drill to the deeper meaning; rather, by not being specific, allow the listener to create their own meaning. The other pattern used above was to keep a smooth flow of language – use lots of joining words, such as: and, since, when, if, then, while, became, even, and, so what.

EXERCISE

Analyse the excerpt of Tony Blair's (the Prime Minister of the United Kingdom) speech after 11 September 2001 (9/11). First look for the precision language patterns, and the questions you would ask to get to the deeper meaning. Then recognize how in **not** answering these questions, Tony Blair creates a rich vision for his followers. (The precision questions are given in the exercise on page 156).

The extract is from a speech by Tony Blair to the Labour Party Conference on 2 October 2001. He has introduced the '9/11' attacks on America as a turning point in history and relates an experience he had at a New York church service two weeks previously:

'I believe their memorial can and should be greater than simply the punishment of the guilty. It is that out of the shadow of this evil, should emerge lasting good: destruction of the machinery of terrorism wherever it is found; hope amongst all nations of a new beginning where we seek to resolve differences in a calm and ordered way; greater understanding between nations and between faiths; and above all justice and prosperity for the poor and dispossessed, so that people everywhere can see the chance of a better future through the hard work and creative power of the free citizen, not the violence and savagery of the fanatic. I know that here in Britain people are anxious, even a little frightened. I understand that. People know we must act but they worry what might follow.'

Answer

'I believe' [*a mindread*, that it is possible] 'their memorial *can*' [*language of possibility* – it can happen] is the message for the listener 'and *should*' [*language of necessity* – it must happen] 'be greater than simply the *punishment*' [*unspecified noun* – the listeners create their appropriate punishment] 'of the guilty. It is that out of the shadow of this evil, should emerge lasting good:' [*a cause and effect* – that the shadow will create a lasting good] '*destruction* of the machinery of *terrorism*' [*unspecified nouns* – listeners will add their meaning to 'destruction' and 'terrorism'] 'wherever it is found; hope amongst *all* nations' [*generalization* – do all nations want this or just nations like us?] 'of a new beginning where *we*' [lost performer – who are the 'we'?] 'seek to resolve differences in a calm and ordered way; greater understanding' [action into noun: that there is such a thing rather

than being a process] 'between *nations* and between *faiths*';
[*unspecified nouns* – which nations and faiths?] 'and above all
justice and prosperity for the poor and dispossessed, so that
people everywhere' [*generalization* – all people?] 'can see the
chance of a better future through the hard work and creative
power of the free citizen,' [*complex relationship*: how does 'hard
work and creative power' allow us to 'see the chance of a better
future'?] 'not the violence and savagery of the fanatic. I know that
here in Britain people are anxious, even a little frightened.'
[*presupposition* – what makes you believe this is the case?]
'I understand that. People know we must act but they worry what
might follow.'

Artfully vague language is at the basis of the power of Tony
Blair's speech. The use of artfully vague language does not imply
the speaker is not genuine. What it does do is to allow listeners
to associate their own experience with the speaker's world.

Three words that stop

> *'Don't try Marge. Trying is the first step towards failure'.*
> Homer Simpson

You have seen how language can have a great effect in
influencing others. There are words that stop people in their
tracks and disempower them. They create a negative state within
people, and inhibit the organization. One organization we
worked with banned the use of all three within the organization
once they realized the impact the words had. The words are 'try',
'can't', and 'but'.

Try

'Try to turn over to the next page.'

Did you? If so you succeeded. Why not say 'Turn over to the
next page'? 'Try' admits the possibility of failure. There is a
scene in a *Simpsons* cartoon where Homer's wife Marge says 'I
like to try …'. Homer replies immediately, 'Don't try Marge,
trying is the first step towards failure.' If you ask followers to
'try' to complete a task by the morning, you have given them the
permission to fail. They can reply, 'I tried but was not able to
…'. Replace try with a positive statement such as 'will'. 'Will'

forces us to think through whether it is feasible for the person asked to complete the task. If it is not feasible, why ask them? You only open up the possibility of frustration and overload for them. If they have the resolve and time, then use 'will'. 'You will be able to produce that information by tomorrow.' If you replace 'try' with 'will' in your own thoughts, you will be clearer about your commitment to succeed.

Can't

'I can't get anyone to understand'.

The can't implies that it is impossible, that you have no further options open to you. If you say 'I haven't yet got anyone to understand', you leave open the options to find a way to do it. You may also say 'What would it be like if you could ...' to unlock possible solutions. Talk about what you can do, rather than what you can't.

But

'I think you have a good idea, but ...'.

Read the phrase above and read this phrase 'I think you have a good idea and ...' Compare the difference in how you feel. You may find the first statement makes you feel less positive. 'But' negates the statement that goes before it: the message that is received is 'You don't have a good idea and I have a much better one', whereas 'and' allows acknowledgement of the idea or an addition to it. Avoid using the soft 'buts' such as 'however': however gives the same message, that you are deleting the other person's idea.

EXERCISE

Stop using 'can't', 'but' and 'try'. Note the difference in the response you get, using your awareness.

Learning for leadership success

This chapter has given you some very practical, enjoyable and fast ways of improving your ways of communicating messages. You have done this by:

- using precision questions to get to the meaning of followers' maps
- appreciating how to be artfully vague through artfully vague language
- stopping the use of 'can't', 'but' and 'try'

09

working with and relating to others

In this chapter you will see the benefits of:
- being visible and approachable, even in a crisis
- giving and receiving quality feedback
- understanding that what you say about others has meaning for you
- working collaboratively to create win–win outcomes

'Cometh the hour, cometh the man.'
(Anon)

'These are the hard times in which a genius would wish to live. Great necessities call forth great leaders.'
Abigail Adams in a letter to Thomas Jefferson (1790)

Introduction

Great leaders do not hide in their offices and avoid interacting with those around them – they turn up in the right places. And really good leaders have a way of connecting with the people when they get there, even in a crisis. They have presence and they use it. Good leaders are able to notice just the right things to mention when giving feedback and guidance to others. At the same time, the ability to listen to others and take on board feedback gives leaders their best tool for gathering information about how they can improve themselves and the situations in which they find themselves. Those that feel listened to and involved feel part of the cause and will follow their leader willingly and with higher motivation than those who do not.

The ability to recognize that what you say about others may have real significance for yourself is valuable. In seeing the truth in this, it will help you, as a leader, come across as being congruent and believable.

A leader's ability to see situations from other people's worlds is indispensable when negotiating for a win–win outcome. By recognising what is really important to the person they are negotiating with, as well as what is really important to themselves, leaders have the ability to conclude negotiations with both parties feeling satisfied and being prepared to enter into further mutually beneficial relationships. Leaders who do not use this approach may win once but their foe (as they may perceive them) will be unlikely to willingly come back for more, and thus a long-term relationship can be lost.

From what you have read so far, you may have discovered aspects of yourself that you wish to change and you may wonder, 'How much do I need to change?' In a recent coaching session, a leader who was about to make a transition from one company to another asked, 'Do I have to re-invent myself completely?' You do not. You will be more congruent and effective when you operate from your real and deeper self. Nevertheless, your development as a leader will, whatever stage you feel you are at, benefit from review, adjustment and fine-tuning. To know what you admire about yourself and to identify the skills you need to develop your natural talents further is a very worthwhile part of your development strategy. Certainly the leader we just mentioned having made the changes said, 'it made me feel at ease in my own skin'.

It is certainly true that leaders lead best when they are being themselves, acting and reacting intuitively and integrating all the leadership skills they have developed.

Developing the role of the leader – things that count

'*If you want to manage somebody, manage yourself. Do that well and you will be ready to stop managing. And start leading.*'

Message published in the *Wall St Journal*
by United Technologies

Jack Welch, a former CEO at General Electric said, 'Being comfortable in your own skin is the best gift you can give yourself … It is up to us to define ourselves and what we want to be.' Welch talks about the need for passion. 'Those who care most, win,' he declares. 'It's about getting into the skin of every employee. It is about imparting energy. Work should be fun, a game, something in the soul as well as in the wallet.' This statement shows the importance of people having a positive reason (a *towards* thinking pattern) to do what they are doing. (However, there are some practices from Welch that are based on fear, such as his policy of firing the lowest 10 per cent of performers (aim *away from* thinking pattern) that in the authors' view somewhat tarnish his reputation as a leader.)

The people around you will also be pleased to see the real you. Welch states, 'You have to be visible to every constituency. Leadership is about being out there.' Woody Allen said, 'Eighty per cent of success is just showing up.' Taking this thought further, leadership is about being seen in many circumstances and connecting with people in all of them. A leader is less effective if only seen when things are difficult. A cry from frontline service workers is often 'we only see you when there is a problem.' This pattern, if oft repeated, leads to the sighting of 'you' being associated with a problem. This pattern is likely to trigger negative internal thoughts in others and will make it less likely that you can create the positive interaction from others that you desire. On the other hand, a leader who is often seen, in good times and in bad, and remains at ease in both circumstances is more likely to be admired as a leader.

Resourceful in a crisis

At the time of the terrorist attacks of 11 September 2001, being seen and being himself was a big part of how Rudy Giuliani, New York's Mayor, tackled the events that followed. He was on the scene at once, a reassuring, capable presence. Being there and interacting with people was the vision we all had of him *being* the leader. The way he was seen to talk with and listen to others at the scene gave the impression that these interactions would influence his thinking and actions following the tragedy. Contrast this with the politician who is kept away from the crowds by teams of advisers and only shown what they want to see. One seems connected, the other seems cocooned. Consider the emotions and feelings that Giuliani may have had running through him at the time. His mind, like everybody else's, would have been full of uncertainty and shock and yet he would have known that letting those feelings overpower him would not have been what was required. He needed to find his own *resourceful state* to do what he needed to do by letting his qualities shine through and inspire others. Recall from Chapter 5 how you explored resourceful states (the Dennis Lillee and Lucy examples) and how to create the right state for any circumstance. You may want to recap on that leadership technique now to show how it can apply to a crisis. Having a resourceful state is a good way for a leader to go out into the fray – even when their personal feelings may want to keep them safe inside or even escape.

In contrast to this there is a story from a high-tech company specializing in Internet banking transfers that was subjected to a hostile takeover by a bank. The bank finally won the day and there was a high level of anxiety amongst the staff. The share price had fallen dramatically and many staff were shareholders. They knew the Bank would not take everyone on, and the rumour machine had started to run. The CEO had a meeting with staff where he attempted to reassure them. He commiserated with their loss of share values, and it became apparent that whilst he had lost money in the deal, overall he would do very nicely through his payouts. The meeting was fraught and afterwards many people wanted to address issues with the CEO. The CEO at this point decided to take a week's leave and instructed his Director of HR to deal with the flack. She did a great job and gained credibility through her connection with people, practical advice and willingness to just listen. He, on the other hand, was described as weak, evasive and cowardly by his staff.

Honing and improving relationships

One of the things that may hold back emergent leaders is their fear of feedback or what people will say or think about them. They target one of the presuppositions of leadership: *There is no failure, only feedback.*

Sir Chay Blyth, a leader in round the world sailing, states, 'Intellectual behaviours are still critical for leaders, but relationships are essential for achieving success. Leaders of today need to be able to deal with people, to build, nurture and develop long-term relationships, show sensitivity, flexibility, and be more prepared to help others to learn.'

The relationships you have with others are crucial. In the past you may have thought of these in terms of how you direct followers' behaviour. Another powerful route to effectiveness is to understand what it is they need from you: what an individual needs more of, or less of, to create the circumstances needed to be fully committed to achieving an agreed outcome, and to be creative in the ways in which it is done.

Creating optimal conditions for generating exceptional and exhilarating performances from others is like turning a key to a powerhouse of talent, creativity and productivity. It makes sense to use it well. A key to creating these optimal conditions is effective feedback.

Feedback: opening the channels of communication

Why give and receive feedback?

Feedback is the receipt of information about what you do. In the past you may have referred to it as criticism and then as either positive or negative criticism. You may even have referred to it as failure. But as in the example of Lincoln in Chapter 4, it is more useful to presuppose that *there is no failure, only feedback.*

We may not habitually step forward for feedback, however it is a great habit to develop. So why is it good to get feedback? At a recent seminar conducted by the authors' company, Fields of Learning, these were the ten top benefits of receiving feedback cited by the leaders in attendance:

1 It will help me to improve
2 It will save me repeating unhelpful behaviour
3 It helps me to become aware of patterns that I run
4 It is motivating
5 I can measure change
6 I know what is expected of me
7 I know how others perceive me
8 I can find out what they really want of me
9 It ultimately saves me time and energy
10 It will increase my ability to influence others

These benefits are powerful reasons to give and seek feedback. Unfortunately people may be reluctant to tell you how they feel about something, and the skill of giving high quality feedback is in short supply in many organizations.

How to give quality feedback

Feedback delivered well is empowering. Some important characteristics of quality feedback are explored below.

High quality feedback is best given **face to face** and when there is **rapport**. Remember that 93 per cent of communication with an emotional content is delivered through body language and tone of voice, and only 7 per cent through the words you use. So the words from the song, 'it ain't what you say, it's the way that you say it' is so true in this context.

And yet the words still count. When you give feedback use **specific examples of behaviour**. State what you have seen the person do, heard them say or what you have felt in relation to their actions. Talk about the behaviour and don't imply any significance to their identity. 'You were 10 minutes late for work on Tuesday' is an accurate statement. 'You are a lazy, insolent layabout' is not! So what has happened in the second example is that the feedback has moved from behaviour to identity and, in contradiction to the presupposition *behaviour, is not identity*. As we discussed in Chapter 5, the effect of an intervention at a higher logical level is more powerful. In this case a concern about a behaviour becomes an attack on identity so prepare for a vigorous response such as 'How dare you ...', 'I am a good worker'. The issue of the 10 minutes' lateness will not be appropriately addressed as bigger issues have overwhelmed it. Be wary of any 'you are a ...' statement as you may be drifting to identity level, which is not the best place to give easily accepted and managed feedback. Stick with the behaviour you observe.

Acknowledge that feedback is **from your point of view**; it is information about how you perceive things. Check what your **intention** is in giving some feedback. Does it have a positive intention towards the other person, or are you saying something to make yourself feel better.

Give your own feedback; let others give their own messages and do not hide behind the 'everyone is saying ...' or 'the whole organization feels...'. Speak from your own position and **own what you are saying**.

Feedback is best when it is **about things that can be changed**; commenting on what cannot be changed is less helpful. For example, how it is helpful for a coach to tell a gymnast that she should be taller! Where things can be changed, talk about what you want rather than what you don't want.

Give the **opportunity for feedback to be two-way**. There may be things *you* are doing that affect the situation. Clarify and use open questions to obtain specific examples of the behaviour the other person mentions. As you do this, be aware of your body language and any gestures you use, together with your voice tone and volume. How would what you are saying be viewed and heard if you were the person on the receiving end? Is this the way you would like to be spoken to?

Feedback should always be **timely** and as close to the event that has taken place as is appropriate. Use your judgement about the right environment, and how much rapport there is between you, but the general rule of thumb is 'sooner is better than later'. Another rule of thumb is 'less is more'. For feedback to be really effective, limit the points you are making to the one, two or three things that will make the most difference. Any more than this and the recipient is likely either to forget, (remember Miller's 7 ± 2 ideas to be held in the conscious brain) or worse, feel oppressed.

Avoid the word BUT: 'I really liked your presentation BUT it would be better if you spoke up more as I couldn't hear everything you said.' As we already discussed in Chapter 8, when the brain hears the word BUT it often deletes all the meaning that goes before it. In this example the recipient is likely not to have kept in mind that you liked the presentation and simply concentrated on your later remark. Just by changing the 'but' to an 'and' can increase the chances of your feedback being accepted. Re-presenting that sentence, you get 'I really liked your presentation *and* it would be *even* better if you spoke up more as I couldn't hear everything you said.'

Feedback sandwiches

The feedback 'sandwich' has been somewhat discredited in recent years and yet there is huge benefit in using this idea if you need a structure to give feedback. Use this special recipe in preparing to give someone some feedback:

- Top layer – start with something specific that you genuinely believe has been excellent.
- The filling – what you can offer that is relevant and can make things even better. Remember, not too spicy or indigestible, and not too much that would be difficult to swallow.
- Bottom layer – something that is a general positive.

You should remember that the development of rapport with the person you are giving the feedback to is the crucial building block. Without rapport the feedback sandwich (or for that matter any sort of feedback) is unlikely to be well received and acted upon.

Here is an example of an effective feedback sandwich: 'The way you talked with the branch managers in the coffee break had a good impact ... you gave them information that was valuable to them, *and* a little less volume in your voice would have made it so much better and helped them to relax more, *and* you are a thoughtful communicator with a positive outlook on work.'

Eliminate the 'but' – make it a but-ter free sandwich!

Giving feedback is rated as being one of the most stressful management activities. Anyone giving feedback – even if it is not done perfectly – deserves a pat on the back.

Receiving feedback

'I keep six honest serving men; (they taught me all I know) their names are What and Why and When and How and Who and Where.'

Rudyard Kipling

How about when you receive feedback for yourself? The golden rules are:

- Remember to look for what you can learn from the feedback you are given, and genuinely listen to what others say
- Avoid explaining, justifying, defending or placating
- Say 'thank you' as this acknowledges that the message has been received. It also gives you time to evaluate what has been said
- All *feedback is just data*: what you do with it is your choice. And remember *choice is better than no choice*
- Whatever you do there are consequences, so you can choose what you want to do with the data received
- Saying 'thank you' to someone makes him or her feel good and more likely to give you valuable feedback in the future

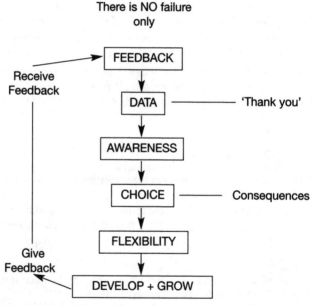

figure 18 the feedback loop

When receiving feedback about something unpalatable, ask 'What would you prefer me to do instead?' This question moves the focus of the discussion to what the individual would like (rather than does not like) and helps you to understand specific desired behaviour. It helps you to gain an insight into how that person sees you. You can use the techniques of precision questioning from Chapter 8.

Use open questions. Questions that begin with How, What, When, Who, Where and Why. Link each of these with 'specifically' to gain even more clarity. How specifically would you prefer to have that done? What specifically would you like me to do, etc. For variety you could use 'precisely' or 'exactly'. Remember to manage your tone of voice and body positioning when asking these questions.

Finally, give yourself time to let feedback sink in. Sleep on it. Say 'I would like to think over what you have said before responding' and a final reminder, finish by saying 'thank you'.

There are some helpful techniques for you to use in structuring feedback you are giving others. These techniques work equally well for feedback for yourself, feedback and review sessions for groups.

More from me – Less from me

How to improve your input into a relationship is a critical skill for a leader. This will be especially true when, as we discussed in Chapter 2, someone is leading in the style of Individualized Consideration. As Chay Blythe says, to improve your relationship with someone ask them what they need more of from you and what they need less of from you. Here is a method to find out that information.

EXERCISE

1 Consider a person with whom the relationship is not what you, or they, want yet.

2 Agree with them a short-term outcome that you both want.

3 State that you want them to succeed and recognize that you could change your approach.

4 Ask 'What would you like more of from me to achieve this?'

5 Ask them 'What would you like less of from me to achieve this?'

6 Thank them for the feedback and commit to the changes you will make for the timeframe you have agreed in order to achieve the objective.

7 Review effectiveness and the difference your behaviour has made to you, the other person and to the outcome that you set.

By carrying out the above exercise you will have elicited a valuable piece of feedback and made a positive impact on achieving a commonly held desirable outcome.

Stop, start, continue

Already you have one technique (the more of–less of questions) for improving the way you deliver and receive feedback. This next approach called 'Stop, Start, Continue' is a delightfully clean way to give 'pin-pointed' accurate feedback. You need to remember to apply all the other rules of feedback at the same time! The following example of Robin, illustrates the method.

Robin is an aspiring political candidate and had been out canvassing with his political mentor Peter. Robin was young, fresh faced and very enthusiastic. Peter was a bit of an academic, able quickly to see wider political impact, with extensive knowledge of political history and with a real sense of what he knew to be right in his rule book. At the end of the day's campaigning and 'door-knocking' they returned to their 'battle bus' to consider how the day had gone. After a drink and a long re-run of the main events, Peter was concerned that Robin could not really 'see the wood for the trees' and that the key pointers that would lead to a better performance by Robin the next day were being lost.

Peter decided to sharpen the feedback: 'Robin, I would like you to stop being so considerate of others and agreeing with everything said; I would like you to start being more critical and analytical, conceptualizing and seeing the wider political point in what people are saying; and I would like you to continue your enthusiastic way of generating ideas for different ways of doing things and continue the way you are supporting me in my role as your adviser.'

Robin now had two specific behaviours to change for improved performance, and reassurance about two other things he is doing well and should continue. Two points are enough to take in; he will be able to see the difference at the end of the following day's programme and it focuses on the two things that Peter particularly feels will make a difference to Robin's performance.

EXERCISE

Imagine that you are going to give some feedback using the technique Stop, Start, Continue. It goes like this:

This is what I would like you to **stop** doing that you are currently doing:

(one thing) _____

This is what I would like you to **start** doing that you are currently not doing:

(one thing) _____

These are things that you do that I like and I want you to **continue** doing:

(two or three things) _____

_____

Think now of someone you would like to give feedback to using this technique, and make a note of the things you would say. Now that you have done this, it will be easier to do it for real and to make a positive impact.

Finally here is a third technique for structuring feedback.

I would be concerned if _____

I would be delighted if _____

These two simple sentences will give the person receiving the feedback the chance to focus on crucial matters.

What does your feedback say about you?

'When you see a worthy person, endeavour to emulate him. When you see an unworthy person, then examine your inner self.'

Confucius

Have you ever heard anyone say about someone's feedback 'Oh she always says that', or 'It takes one to know one'? The following section of this chapter gives some explanation of this phenomenon.

Notice what you notice in others. In particular notice the things that seem to get an exaggerated reaction from you. The things that instantly get under your skin, or the things that you find instantly appealing. What are the things that literally shout at you when you encounter someone else? Look again at the things you have just asked someone else to stop, start and continue.

These may be things that also have a meaning for you. The statement 'it takes one to know one' works on the principle that you must have some way of recognizing something for, or from, yourself before you develop the ability to see it in others. There is so much to observe in others; what is it that we have deleted, distorted and generalized in order to come to this particular conclusion? It may be because we already recognize this pattern or behaviour trait in ourselves. This is known as mirroring.

In the Peter/Robin example, what perhaps is it about Peter's own ability to be considerate of others that makes Peter notice this in Robin? When might this ability be an anxiety for Peter? Might it be that Peter fears losing his ability to conceptualize because he is considerate? Is it that Peter values his own ability to support others that makes him want to see this in others? Is he worried that he hasn't been supporting others lately? What might it be in his lack of ability to apply things in a practical way, that makes a difference in street politics, that Peter might hold as a concern for his own political influence?

These examples examine issues that Peter has noticed. But what are the things about others that annoy or upset you the most? What insight does the mirror hold for you in those reactions?

Because you may be reluctant to acknowledge any negative traits that you despise or fear in yourself, they most often emerge in your relationships with others. This is known as projection. You can also project what you like about yourself when noticing positive attributes in others. You project when you notice or react to some particular behaviour in another person that is really an unrecognized part of yourself.

You may know this is true when you think about how different people see different things in the same person's behaviour. How do you see what you see? It may be that you see it because you recognize it so well in yourself. What have you asked others to stop that you would like to stop in your own behaviour? What have you asked others to start that you may want to start doing more of yourself? What do you already do that you have asked others to continue?

For example, a father was recently heard to say of his son as he saw him riding down the road back to his empty house, 'I bet he is going home to do something naughty while no one else is around.' This perception of what his son may have been going to do is perhaps a projection of what he would have done himself. *Perception is projection.* The mother, on the other hand, imagined that he would go home, hang around for ten minutes, get bored and go out again. That is what she would do. *Perception is projection.*

Thinking about the things you notice in others, metaphorically hold a mirror in front of you and, instead of their face, look at what you could notice about yourself and see how you may be projecting this. The mirror can tell you about yourself and the greatest risk in projection is often that it blurs your view of others, distorting your vision, which in turn limits your capacity to see objectively and relate more humanely. If you do not attend to the mirror, you may not distinguish the reality of your view of the other person through the confusing blur of your own unacknowledged impression of yourself.

Earlier in this chapter we talked about projection and how you can project your feelings about yourself onto others. Here is an exercise that allows you to explore your comments and feelings by examining how you project onto others. Edward C. Whitmont noted that the greatest danger of projection is that it blurs our view of the other person and 'interferes with our capacity to see objectively and relate humanely'.

EXERCISE: Look in the mirror

The purpose of this exercise is to highlight the issues that elicit a very strong response in you, and then to recognize that these may have meaning for you and say something about your own behaviours and issues. The purpose is to hold the mirror up and see your own behaviours and issues and give you some insight into yourself.

List all the qualities you do not like in others; for example greed, conceit, indecisiveness, slowness, sarcasm, rudeness etc. When the list is complete (note that it may be a long list), then highlight those that you not only dislike, but also that you hate, loathe, abhor.

This shorter final list, consisting of four or five pet hates, is likely to be a reasonably accurate picture of your own shadow. As you look at the list you will begin to recognize the things that lurk in your shadow and know that you can face them.

The above exercise uses the principle that 'we recognize in others what we already recognize so well about ourselves'. You may loathe in others what you loathe about yourself.

When you make the effort to recognize and attend to matters in yourself before being critical of others or asking them to alter their behaviour, you are perceived as being more congruent and having integrity. If you say one thing and then do something else, it will not ring true and those around you will see through you and not be so willing to believe in you as a leader. The phenomena is called the '*say–do gap*'. There is a delightful story about Gandhi that illustrates this point.

One day a mother brought her little boy to Gandhi with a request: 'I have often told my son not to eat sugar. I have explained to him that it is bad for him and yet he continues to eat it. I am sure that if you tell him then he will listen and give it up.' Gandhi said he was happy to help but that the woman and her son would have to wait for two weeks and then return before he could help. Two weeks later the woman and her son returned. Gandhi looked the little boy straight in the eyes and said, 'Give up eating sugar. It is bad for you.' The mother said, 'Thank you. Thank you. But why did we have to wait two weeks?' Gandhi explained, 'Two weeks ago I was eating sugar.'

Carl Gustav Jung, the psychologist, explains Gandhi's thoughts when he says:

> '*If there is anything we wish to change in the child, we should first examine it and see whether it is not something that could better be changed in ourselves.*'

So you now understand the impact that feedback can make and have different ways to give beautifully formed feedback to others using several techniques. You understand that the feedback you give may also mirror something about you. Finally, know the importance of avoiding the 'say–do' gap.

The big and little picture: creating collaborative outcomes

Feedback and the information that it gives you will help you in situations where you want to negotiate or agree an outcome. Many people go into discussions or negotiations with a strong position and then proceed to either talk at cross purposes with the other party, or play a sort of tug of war that does not seem to get anywhere until one or both parties give with up exhaustion. Wouldn't it be great to have a way of channelling energy more positively and collaborating to come up with an outcome that works for both parties? The technique for collaborative outcomes can help you do just that.

We were working recently with a business leader, Charles, who runs a successful partnership. Every year, their company has a big Christmas bash to celebrate the year and acknowledge and appreciate each other. His partner, Jacqueline, has traditionally organized this bash and last year Charles felt Jacqueline was disappointed with the gift he had given her as his appreciation. This year they had had a great year and he was determined to get it right this time. Jacqueline just loves presents. But she already has almost everything that Charles can think of. Because he knows presents are important to her, he asks her what she would like. Jacqueline just says, 'Oh anything, I don't mind.' Charles wants his present to make an impact, to be something that will be really useful to her, something she will use regularly and value. He cares about what he gets her and it has to be just right. So, when he can find a spare moment in her busy schedule, he asks her again for some suggestions or ideas. She responds with, 'I don't really mind, as long as it is lovely.' So no hints there! As Christmas approaches, he finds himself increasingly exasperated and, in the end, catches her in a spare moment and suggest three things that he has racked his brain for that he thinks she would use regularly. She says, 'Any of them would be fine.' He notes she didn't say 'brilliant' or 'fantastic' but at least he knew she thought they would be OK. He now felt he could make a decision about what present to get and felt he could risk spending a little more than he had planned in order to increase the impact the present would make. He is very aware of how busy Jacqueline is, so he takes the time to let her know three or four things that he would find useful so she does not have to worry about what to give him. He is good at being thoughtful like that.

At the office party, they exchange their gifts. Jacqueline said her gift was 'nice' (is that as good as lovely?) and she gave Charles something that was very handsome and (he thinks) is a handcrafted paperweight, but not one of the things on the list he had helpfully given her. Charles said how 'impressive' it was and yet was a little disappointed that he had not been given one of the things on his list that, after all, he had set his heart on. So how was it that after going to so much effort, this exchange of presents still was not quite right?

How Charles could have made an appropriate choice is described below, and will help you make sure your choices, whether they are business proposals, tenders, offers of assistance, or presents for your friends, hit the right mark and meet the criteria that really matters to the other person.

The gift of meeting criteria

There was a mis-match of criteria for a 'great present'. In Charles's world, the criteria for 'great presents' are that something has to be *really useful* (and he prefers to be asked what he wants so the present is never wasted). In Jacqueline's world, the criteria for a 'great present' is that it has to be a *surprise*, and it must be kept a secret so at the moment it is opened, all the anticipation and excitement can be fully experienced. How was Charles supposed to know that?

Here is how he could have known. He could have found out Jacqueline's criteria, by using a technique called *chunking*, by going 'up' or 'down' levels of influence. Chunking up leads to higher abstractions and chunking down leads to more specific examples. Chunking across would lead to other examples in different aspects of life.

To ask questions that lead you to a higher level ask 'What is important about that?' or 'What will that give you?' When you ask these questions you can begin to go up in steps to the other person's highest criteria or values.

So Charles could have asked Jacqueline, 'What is important to you about a Christmas present?' The answer would have been, 'It is fun receiving presents.' What is important about receiving presents?: 'There is a real sense of occasion about it.' What's important about that? 'It is great to be excited.' What does excitement give you? 'The shared excitement is the real "gift"! That is what I really want.'

In this example, Charles has now 'chunked up' and found out a lot about Jacqueline's criteria for a great present. There is even more valuable data available to Charles by then chunking down. To do this, the magic question is 'What would an example of that be?' or 'What specifically?' These are examples of the precision questions described in Chapter 8.

He could ask about 'shared excitement; what would an example of that be?' 'Everyone being together and opening presents one at a time with everyone watching and getting excited.' What would an example of getting excited be? 'When you are holding the beautifully wrapped present and imagining what might be inside it. Lots of possibilities go through my mind and the tension builds.' What specifically is the exciting bit? 'The fantastic surprise when you finally reveal the present!'

This may seem a trivial example (although achieving the right response when giving a present seems like a great thing to know!), however the same approach is also true within organizations. This example can help you to see that different people have different expectations from the same generalized words.

When working within an organization we came across a team where team members had very different perceptions of the same leader. One member of a team was telling us how she wished her manager would trust her enough to let her get on with her work without checking up on her all of the time. Another member of the same team said that he found the way the manager asked if he was OK or if he needed any help at fairly regular intervals demonstrated how supportive the manager was.

In this case the same behaviour impacts on different criterion for the two people.

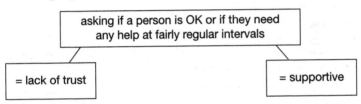

In order to influence others or successfully manage people, you need to be sure that you are operating using 'criteria' that will satisfy their criteria rather than your own. Criteria equivalents are the little behaviours that represent the higher held beliefs and values.

An added bonus of understanding chunking is that you can greatly increase the rapport you have with people if you are talking at the same level of detail or abstraction as them. This is particularly helpful in negotiation or going for a win–win outcome.

Collaborative outcomes: how to win at win–win

Some people's concept of negotiation is that there is one winner and one loser. Stalled negotiations or drastic compromises on the other hand can give you a lose–lose situation. In the collaborative outcome technique you are going for a win–win outcome. You can learn how to create solutions from what might originally seem implacable positions.

In the case of agreeing where two people might want to go on holiday, it could be a win–lose situation where the man wins and they go to his preferred destination. He has a great time (win) and she has a miserable time (lose), or they compromise and go somewhere where they both have a mediocre time (lose–lose) or they collaborate to find a different place that is better than both their first ideas and they have a ball (win–win).

The following case uses the example of a holiday to illustrate the collaborative outcomes technique. It applies equally to other situations and it was the negotiation technique used between the Egyptians and the Israelis which brought about the creation of the Gaza Strip, which underpinned stability between these two countries for many years.

Case study: take time to share what you and the other person want

We recently discussed this technique with a regional business leader who really wanted a two-week break to recharge his batteries. The problem was that he wanted to go skiing in Colorado and his partner wanted to go to Kathmandu and then trek in Nepal. They both had their hearts set on their idea of a holiday and, having done research and imagined what it would be like, both were reluctant to let go of their dream holiday. The impasse was creating tension and he could not resolve it; in fact they were not even talking about it. So we discussed the options. They could have agreed to have one week in Colorado and one week in Kathmandu but that would have been a compromise and not fully satisfying to either of them. They could have agreed on his holiday and that would have been a win–lose result (and vice versa).

He eventually **stated the end in mind** was to have a great holiday. We then asked, 'What do you both want' and got the Colorado, Kathmandu difference.

What is Colorado like? And got a detailed description. What is Kathmandu like? And also got a description

We then asked him **what was important to him** about his holiday? This produced the following list:

1 Being in a wild place
2 Physical challenges
3 Being pampered in the evenings
4 Away from it all
5 Meeting like-minded people

The next question, **'What is important to your partner** about her holiday?' produced this list from him:

1 Going somewhere very different to other holidays they had had
2 Walking in a rarefied environment
3 Proving to myself I can handle a harsh stark environment
4 Having time to talk and think away from daily pressures

As he reviewed the list he noted some similar outcomes they both had on their list. We then asked them to **think of at least three other solutions** that could incorporate all nine important outcomes on the list. We told them that they had 'Carte Blanche' and could be as whacky or adventurous as they like. One of the made up solutions had to be at least as good and preferably better than the original Colorado/Kathmandu they had previously set their heart on. What followed was a 20-minute creative brainstorm with lots of laughter and rising excitement. Their **agreed dream** holiday was two weeks in Australia, sea kayaking, diving and trekking in the remote and beautiful coastal reefs near the Kimberley Ranges. This met all their criteria, and their obvious renewed enthusiasm for the holiday and each other was an added bonus.

The technique for creating a collaborative outcome is shown in Figure 19. It focuses on what is important to *people* rather than what they start by saying they want.

You can use this same technique whenever there seem to be two intractable positions. It is particularly valuable in negotiations to resolve outward conflict.

Learning for leadership success

In this chapter you have learned:

- The importance of 'showing up' and interacting at the right time, place and in the right manner
- The importance of giving and receiving feedback together with some rules and techniques for making feedback a high quality gift
- What you say about others may have particular meaning for yourself
- How to find out someone else's criteria for something to be good
- A process for negotiating collaborative outcomes

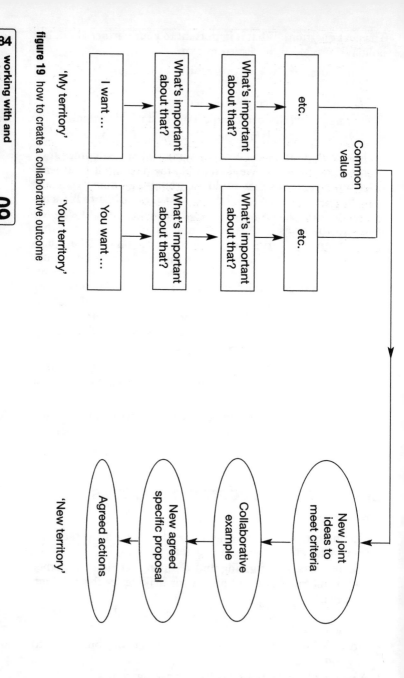

figure 19 how to create a collaborative outcome

'My territory'   'Your territory'   'New territory'

Reflection

And what happened on the holiday? This is the postcard from our regional business leader on his 'Environmental Encounters' holiday in the wilds of Western Australia:

'We have met some amazing people, swum in the unpolluted seas and seen sunsets so clear they are dazzling in their beauty. The challenge of kayaking off-shore and discovering caves with 2,000-year-old aboriginal rock paintings in them gave us both more than we could ever have dreamt of. We have connected with the gentle pace of this remote place with its waterholes, wilderness and timeless feel. The food, support and care from our guides has made us feel safe and pampered. You should come!'

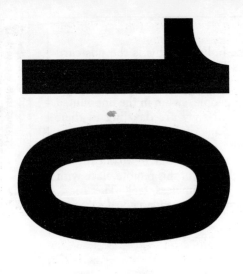

10

balancing leadership and life

In this chapter you will:
- consider the balance between your leadership and your life
- explore what is in your shadow that would profit from attention
- revisit your well-formed outcome constructed in Chapter 3 and make it even more compelling

'They who dream by day are cognisant of many things, which escape those who dream only by night.'

Edgar Allan Poe

'Here lies a woman who was always tired. She lived in a world where too much was required.'

Clementine Churchill musing on what her tombstone might say

'Working ourselves to death? The answer is no.'

John R. O'Neil

The notion of balance for performance

Creating balance in your life allows you to function at maximum effectiveness, like a well-tuned, high performance engine. When you attain this balance you are at ease with yourself, relaxed, able to give the best of yourself and, by doing so, bring out the best in others. Balance is not about taking things easy; it is about being well tuned. When you are balanced and well tuned, then you can drive on to achieve remarkable results. When you are not, you splutter, misfire and leave fumes in your wake!

It can be healthy to gain insight from time to time by standing back, reflecting and taking stock. For instance, as you reflect on the past month, you can ask 'When was I effective; when was I full of energy? When did I have time for a moment to myself, perhaps on a favourite walk, or a cup of tea with a friend?'

You can also consider how the balance (or lack of it) in your life fits with how you want to be. You may be absolutely sure that everything is OK and that if you keep going on the current course it will be fine. You may like to ask yourself 'Is this true for one more month? one more year? three years? five years? until our children leave home? until we retire?'

A common trait of those that lead with ease is a sense of having balance in and between all aspects of their life. The following two case studies from our own work show helpful ways of managing balance. Each leader concerned has their own measure of balance and feels they have it 'right'. You can examine what they have done to achieve this and then examine how you too can improve balance in your life.

Case study: David's system for ensuring balance

David is the leader of his own precision engineering business that supplies the performance car market. He is a busy man who achieves more than most of us. We talked to him about his diary, as it seemed an acceptable material sign of his ability to make commitments and to manage his time. The system that lies behind his diary is unusual, although the diary itself is perfectly normal, and yet it has to be just the right one: it must be small enough to fit in his pocket; it must have a month to view; notes of appointments only get entered; no more than four (or so) things are entered in any day; routine 'stuff' does not get listed. David uses a system of colours to highlight entries: holidays – green; very important things – pink; important things – orange; personal development and meeting up with groups of other directors – blue.

When asked what is important about his diary, he said, 'It's about being in control. I need to feel comfortable. It's good to have good time and balance management. I believe that my ideas are good ones. I used to tend to pack too much in, and now I am beginning to feel more comfortable with "space". But not too much of it, as I will soon want to be doing something again.'

At a single view, David can judge if he has the balance of his life right at any time. He is going for a balanced rainbow with clean white space on weekends. He is keen to avoid:

- too much pink – being overstretched
- too much orange – too much volume, not enough excitement
- no blue – out of touch with peers
- no green – need to plan to relax and do things for family and me
- weekends not clear – doesn't give space for spontaneity and relaxation

David says: 'This strategy applies to big things. I don't put daily things in my diary. I need clearly to see what the targets are. My family have often been displaced by my doing "things" and there was a time when I had loads of "things" to achieve each weekend. I put so much in that I never achieved everything on the list and was, therefore, like a man possessed to get them done, and so went back to work not rested but exhausted and disappointed. My wife didn't like it either. When I have a job to do, I am like "a bus coming through" and there is little sense in getting in my way. I know I have put my family second and I don't want to do that as much anymore. So, nowadays, the weekends are not so coloured. I do things that we plan together, or that just take us by whim.'

Case study: Penny's voice

In her mid-thirties Penny Hughes became the first woman, the youngest person and the first Briton to take on the role of President of Coca-Cola Great Britain and Ireland. Having made a meteoric rise, she was determined to keep a balance between her work and her family life. She said, 'Life comes first but business is a fundamental part of life, and if there were an imbalance either way, I would correct it.' She worked reasonable hours, from 8.30 or 9.00 a.m. until 6.00 or 6.30 in the evening and never took work home or worked at the weekend. She stated, 'Those are my rules. If ever I have a job that takes more time, I'll probably pack it in. It is so important to enjoy life. In fact, I believe that it is this confidence and stability that allows you to do your job. I get up every morning and look forward to work. If I was tired, or making too many compromises, I wouldn't.'

Creating balance through recognition of values

Both these case studies show people who have addressed the need for balance in their life and have done something about it. David values balance in his life and has a visual system of diary management that allows him to check and adjust the balance he needs. Penny has clear values about where work starts and finishes and she communicates these clearly to others so there is no room for different understanding of her 'rules'. They have identified their values and know how to achieve what they want. They understand the rewards this balance gives them. In this section, you will learn how to identify the balance in your life.

It may be that most facets of *your* life feel great and yet there may be one facet that concerns you or does not feel quite right. It may be your weight or fitness, it may be a relationship, or it may be finding a way to relax. You may have a brilliant diet that helps you to stay physically and mentally in trim, or you may be rushing from convenience meal to strong cup of coffee. You may have clear lungs and a strong heartbeat or you may wheeze on the stairs or have palpitations and rapid heartbeat moments.

You will know in your own mind which factors are a concern for you and know that there is a part of you that wants to pay attention to the balance you have in your life. It may feel out of your grasp to change things; however, you are absolutely in control of you and you have choices about what and how you do things that will lead you to the balanced way you really want to live your life. Different people value different things in their life. There are no universal rules, no formulae, only what feels balanced to you.

Values are the things that you hold important to yourself. They are what tell us when we are in or out of alignment. David values achieving his goals in a way that leaves him with energy to face the next challenge. He values holidays, personal development and time with his family to do things 'on a whim'. Penny Hughes also values achievement, motherhood, family life and clear boundaries. She invests in her own health as she values her health and well-being. Your values are how you calibrate happiness or contentment. If you ask the question 'Why?' of someone, it will take you to a statement about their beliefs, for example, by answering the question, 'Why is that important to you?' Then asking 'What's important about that?' will invariably release a value statement. The process of 'chunking up', as described in Chapter 8, shows you how to lift a discussion to a values level. If you can match someone at a values level, you are more able to generate solutions to conflicts, agree new options to satisfy your needs, or develop a sense of mutual belonging with the other person. However, if you try to impose your beliefs or values on another, this can cause real conflict. Imagine if David made it compulsory for everyone in his company to run their diaries the way he did, or for Penny to insist that women give up work on having a child.

Once you have identified your values, you will sift, delete, distort and generalize in their honour! This is is how you make sense of your world. Once you have a clear set of values you tend to sift everything through it, to check whether it fits your way of thinking and if it fits in with what matters to you in life. Whilst our values are unique to each of us, where there are commonly held values these come together to frame the communities and societies we live in. These become shared values. They cannot be imposed. They have to be lived by the people in that community.

The development of values

Values do not come from nowhere; therefore they must have come from somewhere. Have you ever had that experience where you notice 'your mother', or 'your father' just 'tumble out of your mouth'? This is when you catch yourself saying something that did not seem to come from 'your world', but from 'their world'.

The effect of values is interesting. For instance, how many of you have written in this book as you have gone through it, perhaps made notes in the margin, used a highlighter pen or filled in the exercises. Some of you will be nodding and remembering all the little notes and scrawls you have written. Others will be appalled at the idea of defacing a book, and would never even turn down the corner of a page to mark a place. Whatever group you are in, where did the beliefs and values that led to your 'book reading behavioural patterns' come from?

Values are developed as we grow up. Our first seven years are characterized by 'imprinting'. At this stage others can easily imprint on us values that they hold, and we are most likely not to question but to adopt them wholeheartedly. What are the values that you have had imprinted on you from these early years? As you think about them, you will be amazed at how many values that you hold as true come from these early years.

Development in the years 13 to 18 can be typified as 'experiment'. This is when you test if the values fed to you, hold for you. This is when you push to find the boundaries, your time of changing loyalties. Parents of children in this age group will be more than familiar with this. Examples of typical values statements from this phase might include: 'Socializing is more important than education'; 'I am happy, so you should be happy' and its converse 'I am upset, so you should be upset'; 'Who says age or position equals authority?'; 'I am not responsible for other people's wants.'

In adulthood, you refine your values. When you can work, own things and have standards that manifest themselves in all sorts of idiosyncratic ways such as clothes, labels, membership of groups, then you know you have begun to lay out your initial set of values against which you judge whether things are important to you or not.

A workplace example illustrating a values mismatch was of a new employee joining a company. His manager had 'considerately' put together a programme of introductions amongst company workers so that the new employee would meet all the key players in his first week, have a chance 'to get to know them' and be able to establish supportive relationships. As it was, he felt uncomfortable with the round of social introductions, and anxious that he would be unprepared for what he had to do. This was because the new employee valued more highly the need to understand exactly what he had to do in his job, to 'get to grips' with the procedures and processes that he would have to apply and be in a position to be confident that he would not make any mistakes in what he was doing. Once he was confident about that, then he would be more interested in meeting people and feeling that he had something to say to them. Asking the question 'What is important to you about your induction programme?' would have elicited the values statements that would have enabled the manager to match these values and have the new employee feel comfortable about fitting into the new company and motivated to achieve.

Whole of life values

'To put the world in order, we must first put the nation in order; to put the nation in order, we must first put the family in order; to put the family in order, we must first cultivate our personal life; we must first set our hearts right.'

Confucius

You may find that you have different values for different sectors of your life. You may find that you also have some that are true in all contexts. The following technique provides a way to check firstly the balance you want between different sectors and secondly the particular values in each sector.

Life pie

Imagine your life to be like a pie that has different sized slices. Typically the pie might be divided into the following segments:

- Work/career
- Family
- Health and hygiene
- Leisure
- Home or security
- Spirituality and personal development
- Friends/community/relationship
- Travel/holidays/adventures
- Eating and socializing

You will notice that money is not on this list. Money is most often a 'means value' rather than an 'ends value'. If you ask 'what is important about money?' or 'what does that give us?' you may find that it is security, or freedom to choose. It is a means to the more valued end.

We recently coached a leader (Simone) from a leading edge pharmaceuticals company to an understanding of her values.

To ascertain her **current balance,** we asked Simone to draw her own values pie with her own labels for each slice and to divide the size of each slice according to the time she invested in each segment. We asked her to be honest with herself.

To find her **desired balance,** Simone was then asked to think about how she would like to invest her time in the future to balance her life as a leader. We asked her to do this according to what *she* really wanted rather than what she thought *others* might expect of her. This was important for her as she realized that she did not particularly want to spend more time with her wider family who lived well away from her although she realized this might be others' expectations of her. What was important was for the desired allocation to be right for Simone.

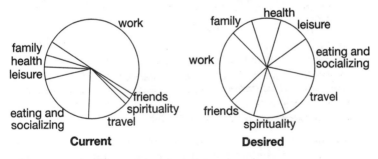

figure 20 example of current and desired life pies

We then looked at **questions to support change.** Simone was surprised that she was already beginning to imagine the sorts of changes she could see herself making in order to adjust the balance. By asking the question, 'What would it take to achieve that shift?' she was able to formulate a plan. When considering some of the shifts, a question that was helpful to remove a block in her mind was 'What stops you from making that change?' or 'What is it you get from the current situation that rewards you – and how else could you have a better reward in your new, balanced life?' (See the concept of secondary gain in Chapter 3 when you were considering well-formed outcomes.)

At the end of the coaching sessions with Simone, she had a clearer picture of her desired life balance by looking at her desired 'life pie' and her whole demeanour lightened as she thought positively about the future. She had begun to see things as she wanted them as opposed to just dwelling on how things were not right.

EXERCISE: Mapping out your desired balance

Now that you have seen the process that Simone went through you have the tools to do this for yourself. Follow the steps described.

1 First draw a circle and map out your own life segments according to how you are *currently* investing your time and energies. Be honest with yourself. Some of you may choose to keep a record for a couple of weeks to really measure this, others will do it from gut instinct.

2 Map out the desired balance you want in your life. Make this what you want as opposed to what you think other people may want.

3 Ask yourself the questions that support change, 'What would it take to achieve this change?', 'What stops me from changing?', 'What gains and rewards do I get in the current balance – and how could I have better rewards in the new, more desirable, balance?'

4 What would be your first step to starting this re-balancing exercise? What little, or big, changes could you make that will get the momentum for desirable change started?

Values within a slice of life

Having mapped out the broad balance you would prefer, how do you know if you have got what you need *within* each slice? Take work for example. How do you know if you are in the right kind of work? You can help answer that question by understanding the component elements that you really value in each slice of your life. What are 'elements' that, if they are in your working life in the right quantities, give you that satisfying feeling of harmony and stability?

Eliciting values

We worked with Simone to go through an exercise to elicit her values for work. Simone chose to call it career, others may call it other things. We began by working through a process that helped her identify what would really be important to her for 'career' to be really good. Later you will have the opportunity to use these same questions to elicit your values.

Label the slice

'In describing this slice of your life, what would you call that? (work, career, occupation, profession, livelihood etc.)'. Simone's response to this was an emphatic use of the word 'career'. It was important to use her own word as the label for this slice of her life pie.

Generate your list of values for this slice

'What would be important to you, Simone, for a career to be really good?' (Simone's responses are in italics.):
'Part of a healthy wider system – it has to be congruent.'

'What else has to be there for career to be great?'
'I need to feel connected.'

'What else?'
'Working on new experiences – variety.'

'What else needs to be there for you?'
'Good relationships at work – ones that grow.'

'When you've got all of those, what else needs to be there?'
'Self-esteem and belief that I can do it', and *'Others recognize my contribution.'* She then refined her statement to, *'Making a valued contribution.'*

Check for anything missing

'If you've got all those is there anything else that would cause you to leave?' Simone answered *'Enjoyment'*, and this was added to list. (There may or may not have been anything to add at this stage.)

Simone now had a list of seven items (remember 7 ± 2 is easily processed by our minds) which she condensed into the following words. These represent her work values and are indicators to know if her current or next job is in line with what she wants.

A 'healthy wider system'
B 'connected'
C 'variety'
D 'developing good relationships'
E 'high self-belief and esteem'
F 'recognition'
G 'enjoyment'

The value of the right order

This list is even more useful when the values are in order. This is because you may be lucky enough to find a career that satisfies everything you want, and you may not. If it does not, having the items at the top of the list rather than the bottom will be important. In most cases, the order that things were first mentioned in will not be the final order. We went through these questions with Simone for getting her 'career' values in the right order.

'Of all of these, Simone, if you could only have one, which would it be?'

'High self-belief and esteem.'

'Is high self-belief and esteem more important than A? Is high self-belief and esteem more important than B? Is high self-belief and esteem more important than C?, etc. (If something else was more important than high self-belief and esteem move it to the top of the list and go through the process again). High self-belief and esteem now becomes A at the top of the list.

We then asked Simone to choose the one on the list that she thought was next important. Simone chose D. 'Is D (developing good relationships) more important than C, etc. This was done until we had checked each item. At any point where Simone felt unsure, we asked the question, 'If you could only have one of these, which would it be?' That choice should then be the higher one on the list.

Check by choice

To complete this technique of eliciting a list of values and getting them in the right order, it is useful to cross-check. We did this by saying, 'I am going to offer you a choice of jobs. One that is with a company that has a clear and honourable purpose and a healthy working culture where you will be encouraged to connect with your ideas and build strong relationships with those you work with (A, B and C on her list). The other is a job where you will enjoy what you are doing and get recognition' (F and G). If you can have one job, and not the other, which would you choose?' If the order in the list were correct for Simone, she would choose the first job offered; if she chose the second job, it might be that the order was not right and that enjoyment and recognition should be higher on her list. In this case, Simone chose the first job.

This list was then of great value to Simone as a yardstick for knowing whether what she was currently doing was a good match to her values. It helped her to see what she needed more of or less of in her current career position and was even more valuable in allowing her to test options in a reorganization that took place soon after in her company.

Checking the list in each segment

Over a couple of sessions, Simone worked through what values she held in each segment of her life pie. This simple process helped Simone bring focus and balance back into her life and to begin to structure her time and energies to coincide with what was of value to her. And when you get that right, work or career, even when it remains busy, becomes somehow 'lighter' and you achieve a sense of balance and harmony in your life.

EXERCISE

This technique allows you to see the values you ascribe to any segment of your life. The same approach could then be taken for any or all of the segments in your life pie, if you wished to do that.

You may wish to ask someone else to pose the questions in this exercise and record the answers for you, so that you can let your mind attend to generating the responses. If you do this exercise on your own, let your intuitive answers come out, as it is your unconscious that can hold the key to this being a revealing and rewarding insight into yourself.

Here are the questions for the technique of eliciting values.

1 Name the segment of the life pie you are talking about (x).
2 What is important to you about (x)?
3 What has to be there for (x) to be great?
4 What else?
5 What else needs to be there for you to know (x) is really good?
6 When you have all those, what else needs to be there?

When you feel you have your list, check with this question:

7 If you had all those is there anything else that would cause you to leave?

Now you come to putting these values for this slice of your life pie into an order. Begin with the question:

8   If you could have only one of these things on the list, which would it be?

9   Now cross-check. Is A more important than B, more important than C and so on, until you have been through the list. At any point if something else is more important go back to the beginning of step 9, cross-checking the new order.

10 You now have the value that is at the top of the list. The next stage is to list what is the next most important thing and cross-check this in the same way as 9 until you have all your values for this segment of your pie in order.

11 Finally, invent two jobs. The first will have a mixture of the top half of the list of values, and the second job offer will have a mixture of the lower half. If you choose the first job, it is likely that your list is accurate; if you don't, you may want to revisit the process above to rework your order.

You can repeat this process for some or every segment of your pie and see where you are getting what you value, and where you are not. This gives you the choice to change what you are doing now so you can get more of what is important to you.

Strategies for change

You already have techniques from this book that can help you make the changes you want. Here we remind you about well-formed outcomes, leadership styles, enabling beliefs, managing your state, negotiating with parts of yourself, and win–win outcomes, and there will be other techniques that also suit you and enable you to make changes. There are, however, some commonly tried strategies that are unlikely to change anything. You may already have tried some quick fixes and you may recognize some of these:

- **Ready, fire, aim**. This is the one where you run out of one situation into another. You may also know it as 'out of the frying pan and into the fire'. This is a strategy that relies on doing the first thing that comes to mind and then hoping against hope that it will work. It fails to take time to recognize properly, face up to and generate more rewarding behaviour options and instead relies on a 'she'll be right' attitude.

- **'Sydney or the Bush'**. This can be recognized as the 'all or nothing' option, when people believe that the change has to be the big one. When people have to do it *all* at once and in a big way, then usually *nothing* is the outcome in terms of long-term change. It is the equivalent of going on a starvation diet, in order to lose weight, instead of examining the lifestyle habits that underpin poor eating and nutritional habits.

- **'Now you see it – now you don't'**. This is a strategy where you announce that 'everything has changed' and you go and find a new job, or a new partner, or a new resolution to do things vastly differently. And yet the changes turn out to be quickly very familiar; old relationship patterns reappear and pretty soon the change is not noticed, as all the old patterns come back into play.

Shiny sides and dull sides

'When I meet people who have had a great triumph, I tell them that I hope it doesn't hurt them too much.'

Carl Gustav Jung

Most of our behaviours have a shiny side and sometimes also a dull side. An attribute can also be a weakness. For example, enthusiasm can also be seen as overbearing. Reflection can also be seen as withdrawal.

You have spent time already in this chapter seeing ways to create the life balance you want and you have looked at the values within slices of your life. The process of doing this gives you a clear picture of how you want your life to be. And yet there may be things that have not been addressed. Things that lurk at the back of your mind or perhaps that you deny publicly.

There may be a shadow that follows your success in leading. The shape of success will be different for each person; in just the same way that each has a unique physical shape. Your success can be achieving goals, or doing a good job in any venture. You can be successful in your marriage, as a parent, in coaching others and seeing them develop, these kinds of achievements are not the ones that are most often mentioned by our society to describe 'success'. It is more likely to be some heady combination of power, wealth, growth, privilege and freedom from daily cares – mythical success.

The concept of a shadow appears in two forms: the 'dull' side to your otherwise shining attributes and the more deeply seated shadows that may exist in your life. The first concept is simply that our approach to some things may not have the impact we intend. We may tip things out of kilter by overdoing or underdoing the way we do things. The second, the shadow, is the dark, vaguely shaped companion that is inseparable from our shape. It can be difficult to pin down and it has a slightly ominous feel about it. If a shadow grows too dark and large, nothing can thrive in its shade. In psychology, the shadow has a more precise set of meanings and can be a useful tool for understanding how the greatest and brightest leaders can falter.

The dull side of the coin

Your character can appear flawed when the impact of an attribute becomes more (or less) than what is needed. You can appear 'out of kilter' when good aspects of your character have been overstretched or concentrated to the point where they tip the balance of the high performance vehicle you wish to be and you begin to misfire. The shiny side of the coin can begin to be seen as dull.

Case study: Manoj

Manoj was a bright leader of a team that ran a busy retail clothing outlet. He had always wanted to lead his team to become the top performing store and he had achieved it with them topping the league ladder. Manoj had now been offered a promotion to a better, bigger, newer store based on his performance. When asked what were the characteristics about him that had helped him to achieve his success, he replied, 'I am confident in my actions, and not afraid to take big decisions. I have made a big commitment to this job. I am pretty dedicated and the success of the store means a lot to me. I am able to charm and interact well with customers and I have a sense of humour and wit that helps me get along with people. I have clear and high standards and I control everything to ensure that targets are met and, in particular, I watch the pennies so we don't go over budget.'

That all sounded good, and yet we needed to question Manoj to understand how things were below the surface: 'Do you think your team are happy?', 'Are you really happy?' surprisingly, No' and 'No' were his responses.

In our world today, the leaders of many successful endeavours experience the joys of high-level decision-making; creativity, motivation, perhaps travelling the world and making things happen that can have an impact throughout a field, across their country or region and sometimes the world. People (especially journalists) will initially create flattering mythological descriptions of them as winners in the worlds of pop, business, sport or politics. They will create a mythical stature that is the alleged form of their success.

As a successful leader, you may struggle in appropriate use of power, relationships, responsibilities, and your own well-being. Or you may not. It is critical to recognize that less desirable aspects of your behaviours may be showing your endeavours in a dull light. It may be that you already have evidence of this whether it be a stress-related condition, tension at work, unhappy relationship, need for adrenalin rushes to keep you going or overwhelming fatigue. It may be clear and recognizable or just a whisper that disturbs you. Some of these descriptions may be recognizable in yourself or others.

So, returning to the case of Manoj, for many people, the items on their attributes list have slipped over to become weaknesses. Manoj aimed to talk to his staff about how they saw his characteristics as a leader so that he could learn from their feedback and make adjustments before he moved to the next step in his career. They did recognize his positive traits and valued them; however, they also saw them in a more extreme form on a regular basis. One of his section heads said, 'Manoj would be even better than he is now if he just toned himself down a bit and trusted us to do things for ourselves. He never considers that he might be wrong, and yet he exhausts himself checking up on us all the time. He is too busy to say we are doing a good job, except when we have to stay after work for one of his team events. I have got loads of ideas that could make us even better than best, but I don't say them anymore after the last time he made a wise crack when I tried to describe what I had in mind. He says he is committed, but that just means he follows company procedures and policies without regard to the impact on us. He can be ruthless.'

The results of the feedback showed Manoj that he was in danger of drifting to the dull side of his desirable attributes. These showed themselves as follows:

Shining form		Dull form	
Commitment	Control	Blind faith	Inflexible
Confidence	Charm	Infallibility	Manipulation
Witty	Economic	Abrasive	False economy
Brave	Dedicated	Foolhardy	Workaholic

EXERCISE

List your own desirable or shining character traits and identify what that would look like if it took on a dull form.

Shining form   **Shadow form**

_____   _____

_____   _____

_____   _____

_____   _____

_____   _____

Confronting the darker shadows

'We are as great as our finest idea and as weak as our smallest obsession.'

Winston Churchill

We have recognized the dull form of attributes. And then beyond this there may be this other form of presence or shadow. At times the shadow may be so well hidden that we do not recognize its existence. You may hide issues well in your shadows and deprive them of light, even deny their presence at all, and yet know they are there. A hidden secret; a denied occurrence; a lie; an action that was cowardly, or a cover up. The things you hope no one will ever find out about.

Shadows affect us as individuals

You will know these darker elements are there, and yet have relegated them from your conscious thoughts. The shadow may be like a large sack in which you have put all sorts of things that are not dealt with, and then drag it around with you in life. The bag then becomes an unconscious snag waiting to trip you up. The chance to empty that bag and lighten your load is of great benefit to you. Every life is affected by the shadow to some extent, and it is a useful way to look at what happens to high achievers who do not attend to their shadow. The shadows of leaders are shown by their actions: leaders in business as discovered at Enron and Worldcom falsifying accounts; in sport,

Hanse Cronje taking bribes and Mike Tyson's violent behaviour; in politics, Bill Clinton's relationships with women, Richard Nixon's lying, and Robert Mugabe of Zimbabwe's intimidation of opposition politicians and media. All of these are examples of the shadow overshadowing their lives, and you will know of examples in your own worlds too. Leaders are constantly told they should show no weaknesses, admit no mistakes, and show no impropriety: be saints, if possible. And then their mythical success explodes across the front pages.

In politics, with such over-scrubbed public images carefully manicured for public display, it is no wonder that politicians frequently disappoint. In general, people who make it to some position of status are blessed with intelligence, charm and organizational ability. They have succeeded and carved a strong ego, and this strong image in turn keeps the dancers in the shadow away from the light and prevents their being cleansed, and thus they wait to trip the player up and cause harm with their whisper of 'that will serve you right for not paying me attention!'

Family or group shadows

As a family or a group you can also have shadows, secrets and names that must not be mentioned. There are organizational and corporate shadows too. The family shadow may contain secrets, denied emotions, or hidden behaviours that affect the dynamics. There may be collusion to cover up violence, alcohol or drug use or other corruption. High profile families, especially those with the trappings of mythical success, may carry a heavy shadow. For example, the Kennedy family, the Milosovic family, and the revelations of the son of the deceased British Barrister George Carman, showed an entirely different life in the shadows of his own home. At an organizational level, there may exist the shadow of corruption, institutional racism or sexism. On the world stage, this typically results in groups being divided into enemies or scapegoats and the Third Reich, the Cold War, and Ethnic Cleansing are all manifestations of collective shadow.

Light onto the shadow

> 'When you stand back and face your issues, a glimpse of light falls on the face in the shadow.'
>
> Rabbi Lionel Blue

So why, then, is it important to address the shadow in your life? Looking back at the idea of the values pie, you can recognize that the way you feel about life when your energies are being invested in the way you want them to be, is very different from how you feel when they are not. When you have the alignment right, you may well feel energy from what you are doing, rather than feeling drained.

You can experience the same boost in your energy and self-esteem when you face and address the matters that lurk in your shadows. You may remember from childhood, or more recently, how it feels to track a lie you have told. The energy it took to remember the untruth would be considerable and may have been better spent doing something braver and truthful.

EXERCISE

This brief questionnaire will give you a tool to recognize shadows for yourself and to shine some light on them.

1 Is your diary saturated with 'important' dates? ☐ Yes ☐ No

2 Do you find less and less time for family and friends? ☐ Yes ☐ No

3 Do you spend little time alone, in fact avoid it? ☐ Yes ☐ No

4 Have you given up some small ritual that refreshed you, like a walk or a quiet cup of tea on the porch? ☐ Yes ☐ No

5 Is competition your primary mode of interacting with others? ☐ Yes ☐ No

6 Is winning central to your sense of self-worth? ☐ Yes ☐ No

7 Are your competitor's losses even more satisfying than your own gains? ☐ Yes ☐ No

8 When your team accomplishes something, do you fret about your share not being large enough or your credit too small? ☐ Yes ☐ No

9 Is your world divided into winners and losers? ☐ Yes ☐ No

	Yes	No
10 Have the trappings and symbols of power become crucial to your self-definition?	☐	☐
11 Do you feel upset if people get your title wrong or fail to recognize you?	☐	☐
12 Are you buying things to fit or bolster your image?	☐	☐
13 Are your trophies shielding feelings of inadequacy?	☐	☐
14 Do you overextend or abuse your natural talents?	☐	☐
15 For example, if you are good at relating to people and getting them to confide in you, do you wind up misusing their trust?	☐	☐
16 Or do you use your skill with numbers, words, memory, or whatever to show off, dominate, or humiliate others?	☐	☐
17 Do you neglect developing your latent gifts because you can always count on the old tricks?	☐	☐
18 When you find yourself stuck, unable to resolve difficulties in your career or relationships, do you invent all sorts of external reasons – bad luck, the economy, other people's weakness or ineptitude – to explain your problem?	☐	☐
19 Do you invariably find your associates or employees flawed and unreliable?	☐	☐
20 When you get bad news or criticism, do you brood on it or take more than your just share of blame for it?	☐	☐
21 Do you dwell on critical remarks or slights, imagining what you could have done to avoid them?	☐	☐
22 Do you overlook and downplay compliments or feel unworthy of them?	☐	☐
23 Has the need for control and the exercise of power become a desperate and depleting game?	☐	☐

24	Do small irritants and vexing details bother you out of proportion?	☐ Yes	☐ No
25	Are you less tolerant of delays, change in schedules, slow service?	☐ Yes	☐ No
26	Are you sometimes flooded with negative emotions that surprise you by their intensity, cripple your effectiveness, and alienate those around you?	☐ Yes	☐ No
27	Does anger boil into rage over trivial events like a car cutting you off or someone pushing ahead of you in line?	☐ Yes	☐ No
28	Have you become rigid in your views and the way you take in information, in what you consider valuable or acceptable?	☐ Yes	☐ No
29	Are you so committed to what demands attention right now that you can't plan for the future?	☐ Yes	☐ No
30	Are opportunities for change passing you by because you can't see them or can't change gears?	☐ Yes	☐ No

Analysing your shadow

You can take the notion of shadow quite literally. The shining form of achievement has a vague, dark companion that is inseparable. If the shadow is so large and powerful, nothing can thrive in its shade. The questionnaire has given you some notion of its symptoms. Check against the sections below how many you scored yes. If you have predominantly scored yes, this may be an area of concern for you.

Section 1, Q 1–4: The whirl of commitments

Do you look at your own diary and see it filled? If you do remember you approved each appointment and you must want it that way. Being in demand is a basic need to be significant. But if you feel uncomfortable alone with yourself, it may mean that you have concerns about who you are and what you are doing.

Section 2, Q 5–9: The spur of competition

A predominance of yes answers in this section means you live in a competitive world where you compete out of habit. You may always need to be on top and you may be concerned about other people's accomplishments. In this area you may be engaged and end up exhausted by a perpetual fight with yourself.

Section 3, Q 10–13: Lack of self-esteem

High scores of yes in this set point to a potential lack of self-esteem and the risk of a fragile ego. You may require external material symbols, such as a large office, to support you.

Section 4, Q 14–17: Over extended talents

In this set you may have a natural talent, such as a quick mind and sharp tongue. As you become more involved you may find that your comments, quick in reply, may become more ascerbic and turn your colleagues against you.

Section 5, Q 18–19: It's their fault

Yes in this set means you ascribe success to yourself and failure to others. You can blind yourself to your own failings. It's as if the magic that made you successful will vanish if you admit failure.

Section 6, Q 20–22: I'm lucky to be successful

When others compliment you on a good job you can't connect to their sincerity. You feel a fraud about your success. You can take on too much blame. Your inner critic becomes dominant.

Section 7, Q 23–25: The need for power and control

If you need to control issues, unacceptable feelings of powerlessness become your shadow. Your habits that served you well in the past, such as attention to detail, may become obsessions that impact on everyone.

Section 8, Q 26–27: Free floating anger

Yes in these areas, means you are angry and the anger may reflect deeply buried emotional needs that require attention. If there is this form of anger, your shadow is calling for attention.

Section 9, Q 28–30: Rigidity of views

You may tend to stick with what works, but to succeed in the long term you need to be flexible and adaptive. As you grow older there is a chance of you becoming more rigid. Do you argue for the prevailing wisdom when someone less powerful argues for a change?

Cycle of renewal

'The recognising and acknowledgement of fear is a mark of wisdom. I call it my black dog.'

Churchill

Have you ever experienced the absolute joy of completing something that you have put off, or shied away from for ages? And then you wonder why you didn't do something about it earlier. A public sector leader once relayed his father's favourite saying, 'Anticipation is worse than reality', and at some level we all know that this is true. The same leader also regularly proposed that you should 'feel the fear – and do it anyway'.

So now that you have a way of looking at your shadow we can also give you a way of addressing what is in it through a process of renewal. In *Paradox of Success*, John R. O'Neil suggests there are four stages in the renewal cycle. We have added a fifth, enjoy the difference (see Figure 21).

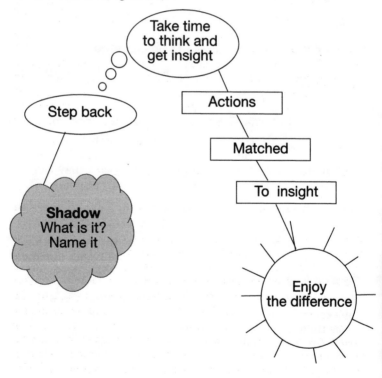

figure 21 analysing your shadow

1 Recognize what is in the shadow
2 Stepping back
3 Deep insight through retreat and time to think
4 Matching action to insight, and
5 Enjoy the difference it makes

Recognize what is in the shadow

The exercises already covered in this chapter present the tools to recognize a shadow. You can add to this process by being clear about what your goal is – focusing on what you want life to be like when it is balanced. Know what that will feel like when it is free of the shadow.

Stepping back

Stepping back has also been aided by the 'life values pie' exercise; yet it is more than that. This is not a rushed exercise. It involves disassociating and stepping out of the groove you already find yourself in and taking a view that allows considered observation and evaluation of what is happening now. Take a helicopter view and analyse what you see from a dissociated and revealing position. Many who allow life to get out of balance do so because they are good at 'doing'. A healthy dose of quiet thinking and strategic vision applied to yourself would aid you in achieving the balance you may desire. At this point, you will have a clear picture of how things look at the present.

Deep insight through retreat and time to think

The deep retreat is about looking inside yourself, gaining insight. Explore the doubts, fears, age-old patterns that do not serve you well, together with the needs and gifts that lie below the surface and beyond everyday recognition. For you to explore fully, you may want to retreat physically. A director of a travel business reported that every now and then he takes a day out and 'stares at a wall' for a while until a clear picture of how things are, and how they need to be, emerges. He says that you have to give the picture time to form, to look at what you see about yourself and to wait until you have the whole clear picture before you. For others you may literally want to retreat for a time; this may be done on your own but for others it may be through executive coaching, by visiting a retreat, or some other activity of self-discovery. Wherever you choose to do it, this process can give you the deep insight you need to make the changes you want.

Match action to insight

Once you have the clear insight about how you want to be, it is time to form actions that match the insight. Sustaining the changes you want to put in place will involve sustained application of the new actions and behaviours you know are needed to succeed in your goal. You will need a clear plan to know exactly what your first few steps will be.

Enjoy the difference it makes

Celebrate the changes you have made by rewarding your efforts with the people that are really important to you. Share the enjoyment of the real you 'emerging to enjoy the warmth of the light'. And before you even start the cycle of renewal you can use your imagination to enjoy what the difference will be like when you make it. Having this imagined outcome and experiencing in advance the joy of the difference it will make when it is done will make the process of addressing the shadows more compelling.

Freedom from or freedom to

Once you have been through the cycle of renewal, you will be rewarded with a sense of freedom. The question is, 'Is that freedom from or is it freedom to?' In Chapter 7 you have already looked at the meta-program or patterns of thinking 'towards' and 'away from'. You may want to reflect that you are in a more powerful position when you are 'at cause' rather than 'effect'. 'She made me feel angry' is being 'at effect', whereas saying 'Why do I feel angry when she does that?' puts you 'at cause' because you can now decide how to feel rather than ascribing that choice to her.

You can be powerful about what you want 'to move towards', have the freedom to do and be 'at the cause' of your own actions. A powerful and rewarding place to be.

You may wish to revisit the well-formed outcome that you created for yourself in Chapter 3 or think, now, what it is that you want from yourself as a leader. Use the well-formed outcome process to strengthen, refine and make even more compelling what you now know you can achieve as a leader.

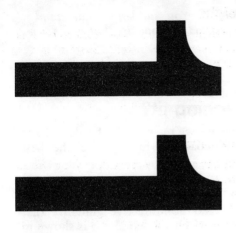

11

leader as coach, and coaches for leaders

In this chapter you will:
- see how you can use coaching to lead others
- learn techniques for coaching
- understand the benefits of having a coach for yourself

'That is what learning is. You suddenly understand something you've understood all your life, but in a new way.'

Doris Lessing

Where does coaching fit?

Increasingly in our practice we see the need for Leaders to use the skills and beliefs of coaching to generate the best performances from others.

There is much written about the differences between directing, mentoring and coaching. The biggest differences are about the degree of directive input and non-directive guidance that are applied. A continuum that helps to explain it is shown in Figure 22.

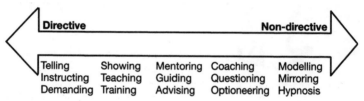

Directive				Non-directive
Telling	Showing	Mentoring	Coaching	Modelling
Instructing	Teaching	Guiding	Questioning	Mirroring
Demanding	Training	Advising	Optioneering	Hypnosis

figure 22 the directive–non-directive continuum

From the figure, you can see that Coaching is a more generative and non-directive approach for getting people to be able to resolve problems themselves, with you as the coach providing support for them to work it out. Not everyone is sure how this differs from mentoring. These are our definitions:

Mentoring

We would summarize Mentoring as being when you have a need to guide the other person to an agreed outcome, you believe that they can do it, and you have some signposts and advice that may help them. You will then leave them to navigate for themselves what they will do and how they will do it. You may check their broad progress and you are available for ongoing advice should they request it. You would only intervene if you saw them going significantly off course.

Coaching

This is when you adopt the belief that *'the person closest to the problem knows most about it and therefore has the greatest likelihood of finding the solution.'* As a coach you will set up a conversation that has a structure that allows the other person to explore the issue for themselves. You create a space for them to understand better for themselves what is happening now and what is possible in the future, and what outcome they really want to achieve.

You create a process where the coachee discovers the answers for themself through your use of listening, questions and models. The coach builds empathy to understand the issue, uses questions to elicit further understanding for the coachee and then to help the coachee create options for more resourceful future choices for themself.

Case study

A Director called Jacquie was ecstatic at being appointed to an Executive Director level post in a large organization. We had worked with her to coach her through the interview process and to help her be very clear about what she wanted to achieve in the post. One of her insights was that she was going to have to manage and lead in a different way in order to be effective in a more strategic role with a wider portfolio.

She realized that she had to find ways of ensuring that people in her area could resolve issues themselves and have an effective way of exploring what the issues and options for action might be. What she didn't want was people expecting her to always have the answers for what they had to do. She decided she needed a more coaching led approach in this area of her role. So we coached her to be a coach! The leadership skills she used most were listening, questioning and guiding someone through a process.

Some of the key approaches we used are described in this chapter. So you can use them to coach yourself to be a coach!

Jacquie now uses these approaches and other things you have read about in this book like Well-Formed Outcomes (Chapter 3), Perceptual Positions (Chapter 6) and the Life Pie (Chapter 10), to empower her staff to find their own ways to be self-directing.

What do you want to get clear in your approaches to coaching?

As you will remember from Chapter 5, where we explored levels of influence, you may first want to look at your **higher purpose** in using coaching approaches. You will decide for yourself, but it may be something like:

- Resourcing this person to believe in their own ability to make a useful change that will develop their potential.
- To help them develop self-reliance.
- To unlock their unique potential.
- To increase their impact in the organization.
- To free them up from the day-to-day repetitive issues.

Draw up your own list that summarizes your purpose in wanting to coach others.

Now if we look at the **beliefs** that will help you coach well, they may include:

- I can help them to help themselves.
- They have infinite potential.
- They have the capacity to achieve what's important to them.
- The person I am working with is intelligent and has the capability to learn
- They are on their journey (not mine)
- They can solve their problems if they have a way of thinking them through.
- I have the ability to listen and hear the whole story.
- I have the time to listen to them. This time is my gift.
- I am genuinely curious about what they have to say.
- Everything they say has relevance to them.
- I will learn from this person.

List your own favourite beliefs that will help you to coach. One of the author's favourites is 'There is an angel in everyone'. This has helped her to coach people through even difficult and messy situations and to continue to search for the thing that will really make a difference so that coachees can learn about themselves.

The skills of coaching

Listening

Listening is not just waiting for your turn to speak! The purpose of listening is to really get into the story that the coachee is telling you. You want to understand it from their perspective. In order to do this you need to listen, judgement free, until you have heard what they have to present. If you build empathy with what they are saying and keep your world out of it you will be a good coach for them.

We recently ran a workshop on coaching and asked participants to come up with descriptions of a good coach and a bad coach. Here are some of the points they listed.

Good coach

A good coach:

- Is on my side
- Listens
- Provides confidentiality
- Is positive
- Gives feedback
- Offers engagement
- Uses a 'whole body' approach
- Is focused
- Gives praise
- Is calm
- Cares about you
- Takes you where you want to go
- Provides honesty
- Keeps you on track
- Practices 'matching'
- Uses 'reflecting'
- Is like a light bulb switch
- Shares experiences
- Makes you realize you 'know'
- Just 'is'.

And the good coach makes me feel:

- That I'm making progress
- Strong
- Confident
- Skilled
- Valued
- Empowered
- That I've worked it out
- Energized
- Intelligent
- Happy
- Trusting
- That the solution is part of me
- Worthwhile
- Resourceful
- Relief
- Part of a relationship/partnership
- Capable

Bad coach

Features of a bad coach included that:

- They were too busy
- They didn't listen
- They talked over me
- They lectured me
- Seemed like they would rather be doing something else
- Kept telling me about them and their stories – 'that reminds me of…'
- Wanted me to do what they had done
- Told me my issue was unimportant (when it was to me!)
- Kept looking at their emails whilst talking with me
- Got interrupted all the time
- Laughed at me
- Sat behind their big desk
- Didn't look at me
- Kept changing my words
- Bored me

Questions for coaching

The use of open questions will help you to unlock what is happening for the coachee. These are 'eliciting' questions and encourage the coachee to divulge more. They begin with: what, where, when, who, why and how.

Closed questions (any that can be simply answered 'yes' or 'no') are only useful when you are checking out the understanding of something. For example, 'Is it that time management affects the situation?' It is useful to use such a question when summarizing back something that the coachee has been talking about. But be aware that if they hadn't mentioned time and organization then this question is likely to be coming from your world and may not be useful in the discussion as it may wrong foot the coachee's thinking and steal the conversation away to you.

Here are some good coaching questions that help to unlock useful discussion.

What . . .?

- What do you want?
- What other choices do you have?
- What will get this for you?
- What is important to you about that?
- What are you willing to give up to accomplish this?
- What are you unwilling to change?
- What can you learn from this?
- What will you do differently next time?
- What can you do to make a difference?
- What is the worst thing that can happen if you do (don't do) this?
- What is the best thing that could happen?

Where . . .?

- Where does this problem happen?
- Where doesn't it happen?
- Where is a good arena to make this change?
- Where are you going to prepare for this new behaviour and approach?
- Where will you be when you know this has worked?

When . . .?

- When does this occur?
- When doesn't it happen?
- When is this most important?
- When is the next time you could do this differently?
- When specifically will you take the step to change this?

Who . . .?

- Who is important in this issue?
- Who do you have these experiences with?
- Who don't you have this issue with and what is different about you with them?
- Who do you want to see you differently and what is important about that to you and them?
- Who can help you learn about this?
- Who do you need to be more like to achieve this?

Why . . .?

'Why . . .?' is a question that can seem invasive and is likely to get you a more defensive response. As a general rule of thumb we would recommend that you rephrase the question to a 'What's important?' format. So, 'Why did you do that?' can become the more useful 'What was important to you about doing that?' In this way you can better understand the beliefs and values that lie behind a behaviour. Understanding and helping someone reframe a belief is more powerful than just instructing them to change. For example:

- What's important to you?
- What will this get for you that is important to you?
- What is important about not changing something?
- What's important about achieving it?
- What is important about what you and others think about this?

How . . .?

- How will you make this change?
- How will you know when to start this new approach?
- How will you learn what you need to do?
- How will you start that conversation and what will you say?
- How will you stop what you are doing now?
- How will you imagine the scenarios that this situation will present itself?

- How will you practise your new ideas?
- How will you prepare to succeed?
- How will you celebrate your success?

Managing your state

As you will see from the Good Coach panel above, the way a coach IS during a discussion has a profound impact. Managing your own state is crucial to running a good coaching session. You learnt in Chapter 5 how to be cool in a crisis and create a resourceful state for yourself. Creating a good state before coaching starts will help you to keep yourself and the coachee on track. You need to get yourself into the right mindset. Being able to switch mindsets is a great skill for a leader as a coach.

Behaviours of a good coach

The behaviours of a coach are also reflected in the Good Coach list above. Your voice tone and body positioning in coaching will be two of the most powerful influences on the impact you make. Both of these can be matched to the coachee. For instance, at the opening of the coaching session, if they are in a high energy state, you can match this with high energy body and tone of voice, and then gradually pace and lead them towards the most effective state to be in to make the shift they need.

The balance of discussion should be with the coachee. If you notice that you are talking more than them it is likely that you are inputting more direction into the discussion and therefore you are likely to have slipped to the more directive end of the continuum. When you do this be aware that you are not really in a coaching mode and it may come across as lecturing, or even worse, becoming boring!

It may be appropriate to make notes within the coaching situation. Wherever possible it is best that the coachee makes their own notes. This helps them identify themselves with the actions agreed, it acts as their own memory jogger for recalling the whole discussion later, and it helps them 'own' the actions.

A good environment for coaching

A confidential space, that is free from interruptions, has you and the coachee sitting adjacent to each other at the same level and with no barrier between you. Access to drinks and the chance to have a break may also help the flow of the session. Clearly defining how much time you have to address the issue helps to keep the focus where it needs to be. You will know this best and yet it is useful to allow at least an hour if you want someone to explore the root cause of what creates the problems they are experiencing.

The PRIDE model for coaching

This is a simple model for taking a coachee through a situation and generating some options for change. It was developed by Fields of Learning for their course Coaching Mastery. (You can find out more from www.fieldsoflearning.com.)

Why is it useful? It provides a clear framework that uses everyday language. It is highly logical and has a step-by-step process. It allows for options to be generated. The coachee remains in control. The coachee generates a script to take away with them. Figure 23 illustrates the five elements of the PRIDE model, which will then be discussed further below.

P	Purpose
R	Reality
I	Ideas
D	Decide
E	Execute

figure 23 the PRIDE model for coaching

The process begins with a focus on the **Purpose** the person has in carrying out their current activity. (The coachee may take a blank sheet of paper and write 'P' for Purpose at the top left-hand corner.) You ask the coachee to clarify this purpose and 'chunk up' to its higher purpose so they can get some perspective on the issue. It also allows them to see if the current purpose has integrity. Once this discussion has defined Purpose and this has been noted on the sheet of paper, the coach invites the coachee to draw a line across and to move the discussion on.

Next you take a **Reality Check** (write 'R' on the left-hand side of the paper). Invite the coachee to describe what is happening now so that they can create a clear representation of the current 'movie' of this situation. Challenge for reality checks and use clarifying questions to challenge their language and get more accuracy. Define the scope of the issue. Once you have this picture or description, draw a line across. Do not fall into what may be a trap of describing the situation endlessly rather than addressing what can be done, which is the next step.

Now get them to generate three **Ideas** or options about what they can do differently (on the paper write 'I'). Get the coachee to park each option as it is generated and then stretch their minds to come up with another option that varies from the first one. A final fourth option can be to do nothing. This means that if they do not change anything, they understand that they are doing that out of choice.

Now they need to **Decide** what they will do (write 'D'). Get them to evaluate the options and decide on their preferred option and actions. They may come up with a plan that takes ideas from more than one option. Get them to be specific. Write them down and draw another line across the page.

Finally, get them to **Execute** the plan (write 'E'). Ask them to clearly imagine taking at least the first step, so that they get the ball rolling. If appropriate set up a report back opportunity for them.

Figure 24 shows an example of a completed PRIDE model. And a blank template (Figure 25) is also provided for your coachees to record a summary of what they discover in the coaching session.

We have described above how the coachee may record this discussion. The process can work equally well with no notes being taken and the PRIDE process just providing you with a template for a structured and progressive discussion. You should do whatever suits the needs of the coachee best.

P Purpose	What is the higher purpose of resolving this matter? What is the ultimate reason for doing this activity? What is the outcome that you want? What are your goals?
R Reality	What is happening now? Describe what you see, hear and feel now. What is working? What is not working? How big or small is this issue? What is its scale? Where does this happen, who else is involved, when does this happen?
I Ideas	Come up with at least three different ideas or options for how you could deal with this if you were resolving it. 1. 2. 3. 4. Do nothing
D Decide	Evaluate what these different ideas could give you. Which one (or combination) will meet your higher purpose the best? What will serve you best and what will it give you?
E Execute	Execute your plan. Imagine the first step you are going to take. What specifically will you do to get the ball rolling?

Can you imagine having the commitment to do this, the enthusiasm, and the motivation to see it through? If not, what else does it need?

figure 24 a sample PRIDE model for coaching

P Purpose	
R Reality	
I Ideas	
D Decide	
E Execute	

figure 25 a blank template for the PRIDE model for coaching

Once you have worked through this model with a coachee, you can encourage them to use it for self-coaching and, where appropriate, for helping others to resolve issues. You can also encourage coachees to use this process as a team assessment of issues or projects.

The authors have used the approach in a Community Development process, and as a way of clients giving feedback to contractors about their performance. Notice how the use of open questions, especially the 'what' questions, helps people to move forward. It is a great coaching tool that you can use to help you lead 'from behind' and let the process help the people resolve issues for themselves. So take PRIDE and use it often.

Coaching for you

Leading can be lonely. Who can you talk to? You may already have a trusted colleague, a peer, a lifelong mentor, teacher or a member of your family that you can talk to. Great if you do, but many people don't have access to this support. Even if you do there are some things that you will want to have a way of working through when the above people are not appropriate. A coach can be like your 'invisible friend'. A good coach can:

- Be there for you
- Seek to understand you
- Know how you tick
- Give you feedback
- Be on your side and by your side
- Help you get through things
- Be your critical friend, challenger and supporter.

The benefits for you could include:

- Getting clear about your outcomes
- Clarifying your vision
- Identifying resources you can call on within yourself
- Creating strategies for asking for what you need from others
- Enhancing your self-belief
- Increasing your motivation
- Getting feedback on how you come across
- Supporting you through changes in life
- Showing you different ways to lead
- Challenging your status quo

- Generating options
- Broadening awareness of yourself and of others
- Enjoying challenging discussions
- Rapid attainment of success.

Different people have different ways of using a coach. Some have an annual contract where they pay to see a coach four or five times a year, knowing they can call on them in between. Some have an agreement to call when they need their coach, some employ a coach to support them through a major change like a restructure or a merger, or preparing for their next career move. Some have employed coaches within their organization once they have felt the benefits for themselves.

The benefits to organizations of using coaching include:

- Self-sustaining change – coachees own their outcomes and actions
- Higher retention of staff
- Hurdles and barriers to success are addressed
- Greater behavioural flexibility
- More proactive and dynamic people who see how to make things happen rather than waiting for things to happen
- Like sportspeople, coaching keeps people in high performance zones
- Work–life balance is addressed for sustainable relationships of the leaders of organizations
- Coaching beds in training
- People who are coached feel the organization values them for themselves rather than just what they can do for the organization
- Good bottom-line return on coaching investment.

A study carried out by MetrixGlobal based on 43 respondents showed a 529 per cent return on investment rising to 788 per cent when financial benefits from retention were factored in.

Learning for leadership success

In this chapter we have looked at the leader in the role of coach, and also the importance of leaders having coaches themselves. We have examined the difference between mentoring and coaching, giving definitions for both. We have encouraged you to get clear what approach you want to use in your coaching of others.

Having set the scene, we then looked at the practical ways of being a good coach as a leader, including the basics such as good listening, and then we developed the PRIDE model of coaching.

We finished the chapter by stressing the importance of having a coach yourself, in your role as leader. Everyone needs someone to talk to!

Reflection

Despina is the Chairman of a world-wide design consultancy that focuses on forecasting the future of work and designing environments for great work. She and her company help clients use space productively, enhance performance, and develop solutions that result in workers prospering rather than perishing in their working environments. This is what she wrote in a postcard to us:

'Happy New Year! Thank you for my coaching over the past year. It has been fun and challenging and it has helped me bring together the different parts of my thinking into an even stronger whole! I particularly enjoyed the exercises that challenged what I need to have in place for the Company to succeed alongside what I need to have in place for myself to be able to deliver it. I have stopped seeing myself as two different people, one that goes to work, and one that does other things whenever there is time left over. I feel stronger in being able to feel more aligned in my life and in my work. We have exciting projects ahead and I feel resourceful in investing my energy into them. In fact it seems easier when there are ways to talk these things through. Thanks and I look forward to more.'

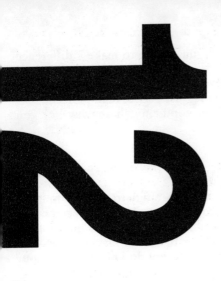

12 freedom from things that stop you

In this chapter you will:
- learn how to remove fears from the past
- be able to tone down a phobia
- focus on the future and overcome barriers to your chosen outcome
- realize you can Just Do It

Introduction

There are many things that you can do to make a difference when leading projects, teams and with friends, families and companies. You could prevaricate and wait a little longer to know that you have everything just perfect (and perfectionists would say that perfect is not good enough anyway), or you could just get on with it!

Getting you ready

In this book you have had the opportunity to address things in your world that you wish to influence. You have been taken through techniques and exercises that give you the tools to address and deal with those things that really matter to you. You now have real choice about what you do in developing your leadership.

Many of you will not need the remaining three techniques that are included in this chapter, and yet for others they will be the most important pages in the whole book.

You may ponder on the state of mind you would like to be in to address issues from your past and get yourself ready for your future. Use the techniques of resourceful states and anchoring to help you get ready to make some powerful changes.

Fear from the past

'He did what he did in spite of his fear. No man can be braver than that.'

Winston Churchill, speaking of a pre-war supporter

It is natural to have fears and often they become part of our make up. These fears do not have to be morbid or extreme. If you do have fears on this scale, they may be almost phobias and we will deal with those later in this chapter.

The imprint of fear

Many people have more general fears that hold them back. It may be a fear of speaking in front of a group, or a fear of writing their ideas down. It could be a fear of interviews or a reluctance to take responsibility.

The experience that contributed to you holding this belief or fear happened for the very first time in your life at a time when you did not have all the resources you needed to deal with it. Subsequently, whenever you then experienced or anticipated this thing, you also experienced it as fearful. Now every time you encounter a similar situation you put the label of fear on it. Being fearful reinforces the fear and just adds to the whole unhelpful cycle you have set up. You will now be given a technique that will help you to address those fears, giving you the choice to change.

Timelines

The idea of creating a timeline to walk along is a helpful notion and technique for exploring time and feelings and experiences associated with those times. The first stage of timeline work is to identify where you experience your past. It can be good fun to just close your eyes and point in the direction you think represents your past. Do the same for the direction of your future. You will be amazed at the different ways different people can experience this.

For these timeline exercises, we will also be asking you to identify a line on the ground, establishing which direction is past and which is future and where, on the line, the present is. To use the timeline you will also be using the techniques of perceptual positions, and association and disassociation (both from Chapter 6).

Many of us have experiences from the past that have a lasting impact. It is possible for an experience to subconsciously inhibit us in subsequent years. Examples may be where we say, 'Well I never have been able to do ...', or 'When faced with ... I always ...' These are known as *limiting beliefs*. Timelines can help by reframing experiences that initiated the original belief.

Case study: Graham

We recently coached a senior manager in the public sector. He was experiencing real difficulties motivating his team. They had been working very hard, yet it was all too dour and serious. He wanted to be able to lighten up a little at work and encourage others to enjoy their days too. Graham was looking for lightness and joy as well as wanting to maintain the hard work rates that were already going on. Yet, he just did not believe that he could create this feeling for his team. He said, 'I never was able to have fun', ' I am always the responsible one that ensures we get to the finish line.' 'Boring but dependable – that's me.' Yet he didn't want to be like that. We asked him to work on a timeline to change the belief that he was always boring and dependable. We identified a timeline on the ground; the past was in one corner of the room and an imaginary line then stretched across the room. Then, standing in a different part of the room we reminded Graham of a time when he had been resourceful, a time that he described as 'chilled and strong'. We anchored this resourceful state with the words 'chilled and strong' and with a squeeze on his elbow using the resourceful state technique in Chapter 5. Anytime in this process when he needed to feel chilled and strong he could break off from the exercise and come to this resourceful 'chilled and strong' place. We informed Graham that when he stepped onto the timeline he was to be fully associated (first position) into the experiences he was going to have. At any time he wanted to step off the line he could and at this point he would disassociate (third position) from what he was experiencing. If he needed to access his resourceful state he could also step off the line and go and visit 'chilled and strong'. If he wanted to take a break at any point he could do that too.

Then we asked Graham to step onto his timeline at the 'present' and bring to mind his limiting belief that he was 'boring but dependable'. Graham was then asked to turn and face his past and step back identifying the most recent significant time when he had experienced this belief. It was about two weeks prior. We asked him to associate into that experience. It was up to him if he chose to tell us about any of the experiences, and it would also be helpful if we had some marker (for example he talked of getting ready for the Annual Meeting in the evening). Once we had made a note of his experience we asked him to move back down his timeline to time before that when this feeling was a significant factor. This one was about 18 months earlier and the team was working hard to complete a comprehensive spending review. He re-experienced this time again and was able to tell us what it felt like to be boring but dependable and when he was ready he moved on to the next significant incident of this feeling in his past. It was after a conference, in a bar, when he had agreed to be the driver for the group on a night out and therefore had refrained from drinking.

We carried on until he had re-experienced being at College when everyone was preparing for their finals; at school when he was a school counsellor; and finally back to a time when both parents were working and he had to collect his siblings from school each day and walk home with them and get them their tea. We asked him if there was anything before this, and although he didn't think there was we suggested that he just take a step to see if there was.

As he stepped forward he realized that there was a time when he was aged about five and his mother had been very ill after the birth of his littlest sister and he had had to look after the middle brother, who was then three, for quite long periods every day. He said this was very hard work. He wasn't sure what he had to do and yet he knew it was really important to keep everyone safe. He worried about his brother getting into mischief, his baby sister crying, his mother crying and the fact that when his dad came home from work each evening he seemed cross and angry. He said it was very hard work keeping everyone together and safe and happy. We checked again if there was anything before this, and this time there wasn't.

At this point we asked him to step off the line into a neutral space and to disassociate from the experiences. It had clearly been quite a moving and enlightening journey that had taken about 15 minutes in real time and yet his recollections were fully from more than 35 years in the past.

The next important part of this technique was to ask Graham to identify the significant other people involved in this earliest experience. At this point we wanted him to stay in disassociated third position, as if a distant observer. Once he had identified these people – he identified three, his mother, his father and a friendly neighbour – we identified three spaces to represent each of these people. He stepped into their shoes one at a time (associated second position), identified what life was like for them at that time and pinpointed the resource they would have needed (to deal with that situation differently). Mother – awareness that he couldn't manage all he was being asked to do and the ability to ask for help from others. Father – understanding that five-year-olds need to have fun and be reassured too. Neighbour – to overcome her shyness and offer to help and support.

We then walked back parallel to his timeline to the spot he had called 'the present' and asked him to step back on as himself, adult, now. We asked him to look back down the line to his younger self trying to manage all that he was doing. We asked the adult Graham to identify the resource that would have been helpful to him at the time he was five. He chose to offer the resource of having the courage to ask his parents for help, perhaps from his neighbours or relations, so he could also have times when he could go out and play and relax and be five. The resource he needed was courage to ask for help. Graham then sent that resource of courage to his younger self.

Next we asked him to send the gift of the resources the other three needed: Mother, awareness; Father, understanding of five-year-olds, Neighbour, overcoming shyness. Graham was asked to imagine these people accepting these gifts and therefore being more resourceful now.

We stepped off the line or 'the present' and walked beside it back to the time he was five where he stepped back onto the line and accepted this resource of the courage to ask for support and time to enjoy himself. He did this. At this point, as we watched Graham, his state lightened and he seemed less tense, and we noticed him smile a broad smile as we asked him to re-experience the earliest moment *with* this resource in play.

Now, and this is the best bit, we asked Graham to step back onto the line and re-live the experience with all the new resources in play. We saw him smile, laugh a little, and visibly relax. We then asked him to walk back up the line, stopping at each of the significant experiences he had talked about and re-live them and experience how they were different now those resources were available and the previous experience was different. When he got to the present, he was relaxed, seemed amused at how different the experiences now were that he was enjoying it and having others share responsibility.

We asked him to step off the line and bring to mind the next situation he could imagine where he wanted some purposeful fun. He then stepped back onto the line, faced the future with all his resources in play and stepped into the experience. He was chuckling out loud, smiling and nodding, as he was now able to experience this genuinely being fun and could see how he could create this outcome.

We asked him to step back into the present, step off the line and told him that the session was over and he could now look forward to lots of fun and enjoyment in his future.

As an exercise we have outlined the process in a way that you could use it to coach someone else through the process. It is a rewarding and life-changing experience.

EXERCISE: Freeing people from persistent limiting beliefs

This technique can also help you to help others. The exercise below is based on you using the skills and techniques that you have acquired throughout this book to coach others through the process. The trick is to manage the process and allow the other person to deal with their own issues. You can use this technique without knowing what the subject matter is. You do not need to know. At no point should you offer advice or solutions. You do need to use your skills of rapport, creating a resourceful state for someone and being able to anchor it, matching, leading, sensory acuity, perceptual positions, flexibility, intuition, and staying with the desired outcome so that the process will lead to the person being in a more resourceful position. As a technique, it requires a little time (an hour or so), some privacy and the person knowing they are in control at every point. At whatever point you conclude, the person will have some valuable insight and learning about what makes them 'tick' and how they can 'tick' in the way that they want to in the future.

1 Anchor a resourceful state.
2 Identify a limiting belief (which may be established by talking about an unwanted behaviour).
3 Establish the direction of their timeline.
4 Ask them to step onto the timeline at the present and facing the future.
5 Ask them to bring the limiting belief to mind again.
6 Turn to face the past and walk back identifying (significant) times when you experienced situations impacted by the belief.
7 They continue to step back as early as possible until they can remember no more experiences. At this point, encourage them just to go back a little bit more to be sure there really are no more. If there are not they should walk forward again to the earliest experience, and then step off the timeline into a neutral area.

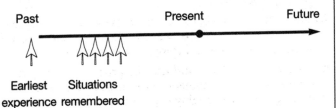

Past   Present   Future

Earliest   Situations
experience   remembered

Figure 26 a timeline

8   From this neutral point (third perceptual position) help them to recall all the significant people involved in the situation. You need to be sure they remain as if a distant observer, i.e. in third position.

9   With each person identified, they should step into each of these significant people's 'shoes' (second perceptual position). Then, step off the timeline and break state in between each.

10 With this second position experience in mind, ask them to identify what resources each of those people would have benefited from had they had them at the time.

11 Walk parallel to the timeline back to present. From present, look at the young self and identify the resource that would have been helpful to them at that time.

12 From present, send the resource to the young self and see them being accepted.

13 Send resources to each of the other significant people and see them being accepted.

14 Walk back parallel to the timeline, stepping on to the timeline as the young self.

15 Allow them to re-live the earliest experience with all the new resources in place. Once this new experience is achieved, encourage them to walk forward towards the present stopping at each of the previous events and experience them in a new way. They may want to talk about how it now feels so different.

16 And then encouraging the new belief and feelings to be built, step into the future to the next likely similar situation with all the resources in place. Now get them to describe how much better that scenario can now unfold.

17 Return to present, and then step off.

You might see timelines presented in different ways. As with any technique each of these approaches may be effective. We are offering our preferred recipe on the basis of our experience.

Managing a phobia

There are some limiting beliefs that are so powerful that the idea of directly reliving or re-associating into them is not recommended lightly. And yet because the brain has set up in some way this intense fear or reaction it can also set it in a different way that is more enabling.

The following technique is one we use with all sorts of people. It is known as 'fast phobia cure' and it does what the label says. It works with the metaphor of going to the movies.

We recently coached a group in this technique by demonstrating how you could tone down an irrational and debilitating fear. In the demonstration case it was someone being phobic about being alone in the dark. You can imagine how limiting that was for the person involved. By the end of the session using the technique described, whilst she may not have been completely at ease in the dark on her own, she was nevertheless able to imagine herself managing in most situations and this alone had allowed her to make choices she otherwise would have avoided.

The fast phobia cure technique

1 Establish a resource anchor. This is just to use should your 'client' want to break state from the process at any point.

2 Establish what fear/phobia they would like to change.

3 Acknowledge to the client the mind's ability of one-trial learning, and how the brain has learnt from one occasion to always have this fearful reaction. The great news is that the brain can now learn to have another reaction.

4 Imagine a blank movie screen. Ask the client to come into the theatre, sit down in disassociated third position and see a still frame black and white image of their younger self on the screen at a time before the onset of the bad memory. They see a time when they felt safe and secure.

5 Next, ask the client to dissociate once more from their body and come to an imagined projection booth. As they enter the projection booth the client can now see themselves in the auditorium, looking at a black and white picture of their younger self.

6 Tell the client they are going to run the black and white movie all the way through until they reach a time after the event when they know they were safe and secure. The client watches themselves watching the movie and experiences a

double dissociation from the memory. They watch themselves watching the movie. They are not directly watching the movie.

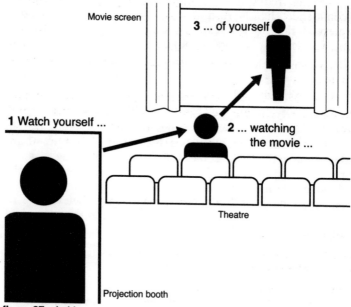

figure 27 phobia cure

7 Ask the client to freeze-frame at the time after the event when they were safe and secure. Now ask them to blank the screen.

8 Now ask the client to run the movie backwards this time, in colour, at speed. Do it really fast in a few seconds. It will be like a silly cartoon, until they get back to the safe point before it started. Anchor this process with either a 'whiiiiiish' or some sound you make. They might want to make the backwards soundtrack noise themselves.

9 Always starting at the blank screen and only ever running the film backwards repeat the process three to five times. It may now have become really amusing. Your aim is to get them to re-print this memory as funny and laughable. To anchor these new feelings to that memory.

10 Test and future pace. Ask them now to imagine going into a situation again (like going into the dark), and calibrate their response. If they are still experiencing a disabling reaction, go back and repeat the process until their feelings/kinesthetic reaction disappears or is manageable.

Following this coaching session, the participants coached each other through the technique. There was an extraordinarily interesting case of a woman called Jan who had an irrational fear of horses. It meant she could not relax when in country lanes, was uneasy if police or ceremonial horses were present and absolutely would turn down hospitality opportunities like the races, polo, ceremonial occasions. It did not help her in her role, which included representing her company in a public relations capacity.

She was coached by Fiona from the group through the fast phobia cure technique and was also able to visualize herself coping, if not loving, future occasions where horses might be evident. Well done Jan, and her coaches, for overcoming in 20 minutes what had been limiting her for a lifetime.

Moving on – making choices

Three wise steps

A leader once described moving on and doing things as coming down to three factors:

- Knowing what you want to do
- Knowing how to do it
- Creating the chance to do it

These are three factors in creating the things you want to achieve. You might want to consider the well-formed outcome that you had the chance to formulate in Chapter 3, which will have clarified for you exactly what you want to do. If it does not yet feel compelling then your well-formed outcome may benefit from a revisit to fine-tune it a little bit more. The 'knowing how to' bit does not mean that you have to have pre-plotted every step. To plot every step is likely to be a waste of your resources. However, you may be aware of the behaviours and skills you need to have in place, but more importantly the beliefs that will support you doing all the things you have to do to achieve your outcome. And then you must take on the identity of yourself as a person that is already achieving these things.

You will need to create the 'chance to DO' the things you want to achieve. Don't hear yourself saying in a year or two 'I always wanted to achieve … But I somehow never got the chance to.' Take control, make it happen and give yourself the chance to be the leader you can be for the cause you dream of.

Time to choose

Future timelines

This technique is a culmination of much that you have learned in this book and it will bring your future choices clearly into view and enable you to make the decision that will be right for you in achieving a significant outcome that you want.

In working through this technique you will be using the skills of outcome thinking, resourceful states, anchoring, and enabling beliefs. You will consider the leadership styles that are needed at different stages and you will really experience the 'you' that you need to be to achieve the things that you really want to achieve.

Case study: Anna

First a story from our practice. Anna was facing some life and some career changes. We worked with her through a process called future timeline choices. Anna was uneasy about the direction that her life was going in. She had a sense of treading water and underachieving compared with what she felt, at some deep level, she could really do in life. She was coasting and using up time. We agreed to work with her and, as it was a sunny day, chose a park as our venue. In the park we asked Anna to generate at least three different options for the future outcome she wanted. In Anna's case it was a change of career direction. She had an idea – and we told her that was all it was, 'an idea'. We encouraged her to imagine another one, which she did after some encouragement, to create a radically different idea to her first one. She came up with one and we informed her that now that she had two ideas she was the proud owner of a 'dilemma'. If she really wanted options she should dream up another option and make it very compelling. OK, now that she had three ideas she officially had 'options'.

In the park we got her to agree a spot that she was happy to label as 'now'. We asked her to step into now and tell us what it was like. This Anna did and out came her feelings of 'wasting energy' whilst she 'treads water'. A sense of keeping doing what she was doing because she had never paused for long enough to see how it could be different. Her posture was tense, her sentences short and staccato and her breathing shallow. She was doing a pretty good impression of someone being agitated and impatient with herself.

We then asked Anna to step off her spot labelled 'now', and to identify three different landmarks in the park to signify the three options she had come up with. She chose a willow tree, a huge cedar tree and a hedgerow.

Anna was asked to think of achieving her first option or outcome and begin to describe it in as much detail as she could. She would throughout this remain in disassociated third position. We asked her to concentrate on what it would be like if this option worked really well. Imagine the type of things that would be going on when this option is working really well, what she would see happening to her, what she would hear, and how she would see herself reacting in this position and achieving this outcome. Once she had a representation of what this would be like we asked her to name it and she chose 'staying where I am with changes'. Anna then chose which landmark she would like to have this option be. She chose the cedar tree.

We then walked up to the cedar tree and agreed a particular spot on the ground beneath it. Then we asked her to step into 'staying where I am with changes' and really associate and experience how good it could be. What would she see, hear and feel? As she did this she talked about what it would be like in some detail. (This may not always happen and some people may prefer to keep silent. That is fine – as a coach leader you do not need to know the detail, as a subject you will already know what is happening in their imagination!) When Anna had fully experienced this we asked her to step off the spot and we wanted her to think about something else so we asked her to tell us what colours she was wearing yesterday. This broke her state and allowed her to clear her mind of her thoughts about option one.

We walked briskly back to the spot we had identified as 'now' just making small talk. When we arrived at 'now' we asked Anna to go through exactly the same process as above for options two and three, and we visited the willow tree for 'living and working in another country' and the hedgerow for 'being a freelance consultant and adviser'. These were not just wild whims. She has dual nationality with Canada, and she had done a short stint of consultancy work in the past.

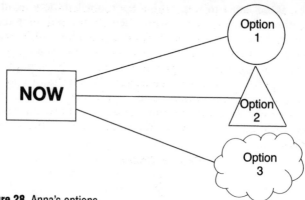

figure 28 Anna's options

When Anna had completed experiencing all three options. We went back and stood in the 'now' spot and let her know she now had four options – the do nothing and stay in the 'now', the 'cedar tree', the 'willow' and the 'hedgerow' – and that she could choose the one that felt the best. It made us all chuckle at this point as she just did not want to stay in the 'now' at all and was hopping from foot to foot as if trying to avoid that all costs. She then clearly strode towards the willow tree and her option of 'moving to another country'. This was the option we were now going to work on in more detail. Not that the others were not possibilities, but this was the option to which she was going to apply her focus.

The next part of the process is quite procedural and we recorded quite a lot of detail of what Anna said. We do not reproduce all that here, but give a brief outlines of the process.

Anna came back and stood briefly in the 'now' spot and we asked her to imagine a timeline from now to fully achieving her outcome of 'living and working in another country'. She also decided that this outcome was probably twelve months away. Once she had this all set in her mind, we asked her to step forward along her timeline to achieving working and living in Canada and to stop as soon as she encountered a barrier or a difficult situation. We asked her where this was, and what it was. She replied, telling family she wanted to go to Canada. We asked her to tell us what resources (internal resources) she would need to get through this barrier. She said 'clarity of thought' and 'good communication.' We asked her to step off the line to the right and recall a time when she had just the right sort of 'clarity of thought', and asked her to re-experience that.

We then asked her to do the same for 'good communication' (This is a similar process to resourceful circles and anchoring techniques.) Once Anna had fully associated with these experiences and resources, we asked her to step back onto the line with those resources in play and to tell us the actions she was going to take to get over the barrier. This technique works by mapping both resources and significant actions. She associated herself into doing these actions – a sort of mental rehearsal of it going really well. We made a note of the actions she described.

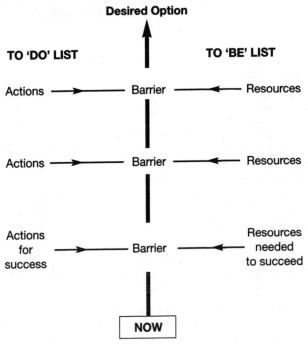

figure 29 Anna's timeline

We repeated this process all the way up to the achievement of her desired outcome. The last part of the timeline got faster and faster as she realized she could easily achieve it with all these actions in play. When she got to the willow tree she again stepped into it being really good. We then asked her to turn and look back down her timeline and recognize all that she had achieved to reach this point.

Finally she walked parallel to her timeline and back to her 'now' and we just re-imprinted the resources and actions she needed. She then took the notes and did this a couple of times for herself until she felt she knew this journey very well.

In essence this completed the technique, and yet we wanted her to really bed it in so we asked her to use her notes to write up the timeline in her own hand, together with the resources and actions she needed. The homework also included her writing out, preparing for and rehearsing her first step, which you may recall was about 'clarity of thought' and 'good communication' and telling her family about it. Once she got started we knew she would be on her way to achieving her chosen future outcome using a forward timeline.

EXERCISE

Here is the technique for forward timelines for your own use, or to coach someone else through this remarkable process.

1 Generate three or four outcomes/options for the future.
2 Find an open space or large room and identify a spot for now, and a location that represents each option.
3 Step into 'now' and associate with how things are at present.
4 Step off 'now' and begin to describe one of your options from a disassociated perspective.
5 Decide which landmark represents this option and walk to this place and identify an exact spot that will represent this option being achieved.
6 Step into this spot and fully associate with the experience of this option being achieved and being really good. Take time to get the full experience.
7 Step off the spot, break state and walk back to the 'now'.
8 Repeat steps 5 to 7 for each option.
9 Step back into 'now' and choose which option is the most compelling or feels best and walk towards it. Step into it when you reach its spot and experience it again.
10 Walk back to 'now' and designate a timeline between 'now' and the location of the desired outcome.
11 Step onto the line at 'now' and begin to walk on the timeline towards your outcome until a barrier/hurdle is perceived. Identify the internal resources you would need to get you through this barrier. Step to the right of the line and recall a time when you had this resource and associate into that

resourceful experience. Step back onto the line *with* resources and describe the actions to be taken. Record these actions and resources.

12 Continue to step forward along the timeline to identify barriers, resources and actions (at each barrier repeat step 11). Record each barrier until the outcome is reached and again step into it and experience it fully.

13 Now step out of that experience and walk back parallel to the timeline and repeat steps 11 and 12 using notes as a prompt. Do this as often as you want, a minimum of three times.

14 Homework. Write up the journey, barriers, resources and actions in your own hand and words. When this is done, write up the first actions (with the resources in play) to be taken in detail and have a very clear plan of what you want to do, how you are going to do it and how to get the chance to do it.

Enjoy the motivation and momentum that flows.

Go and do what you want to do

Throughout this book you have discovered ways of achieving what you want for yourself, for your cause, and you have explored ways as a leader that you can achieve amazing results. You have your well-formed outcome from Chapter 3 together with the resources and techniques to make this really compelling. You can increase you effectiveness by layering all the insights, techniques and the personal learning and discovery you have had on top of your well-formed outcome to make it invincible if that is what you want. So you have taught yourself – now go and do it and enjoy your journey!

Reflection from Jan

Remember taking me through my fast phobia cure on horses. Well I am pleased to say it has now been well and truly tried and tested. I went to the races on Saturday at Newbury and not only watched the races but went to the parade ring and then stood by the railing as they were ridden out. I was a bit nervous at the last bit but only a little bit. Last year when I was asked I couldn't even contemplate getting in the car to go to the races and certainly wouldn't have gotten out of it at the other end.

So thank you, I had a lovely day out although they did look a bit funny running backwards to the starting line! Love. Jan

taking it further

The sources listed below were used in preparing this book, and we also use them as inspiration for our work. You may like to investigate them to support the development of your leadership skills.

Bailey, Roger (1991) *Hiring, Managing, and Selling for Peak Performance.*

Bass, Professor Bernie, and Avolio, Bruce (1987) 'Biography and Assessment of Transformational Leadership at the World Class Level', *Journal of Management*, Vol. 13, 1 March.

Bavister, Steve, and Vickers, Amanda (2004) *Teach Yourself NLP*, London, Hodder Education.

Bodenhamer, Bob, and Hall, Michael (1999) *The User's Manual for the Brain.* Crown House Publishing, Carmarthen.

Dilts, Robert B. (1996) *Visionary Leadership Skills: Creating a world to which people want to belong.* Meta Publications, Capitola, California.

Hall, Michael, and Bodenhamer, Bob (1997) *Figure out People: Design Engineering with Meta-Programs.* Crown Publishing, Carmarthen.

Kahili King, Serge: websites at www.king.org and www.sergeking.com.

McMaster, Michael, and Grinder, John (1993) *Precision: A new approach to communication.* Grinder, Dehazier and Associates, Portland, OR.

Morrell, Margaret, and Capparell, Stephanie (2001) *Shackleton's Way: Leadership lessons from the Great Antarctic Explorer.* Nicholas Brearley Publishing, London.

O'Connor, Joseph, and Seymour, John (1993) *Introducing Neuro-Linguistic Programming: Psychological skills for understanding and influencing people*. Thorson, London.

O'Neil, John R. (1993) *The Paradox of Success*. McGraw-Hill, London.

Shackleton, Sir Ernest (1999) *South: the Endeavour Expedition*. Penguin Books, London.

Shackleton. A First Sight Film Production for Channel 4. Available from Channel 4 shop: www.Channel4.com.uk/shop, or 00 44 (0) 870 123 4344.

Tad, James (1990) *The Basic NLP Training Collection*. Advanced Neuro Dynamics University, Honolulu, Hawaii.

Vickers, Amanda, and Bavister, Steve (2005) *Teach Yourself Coaching*, London, Hodder Education.

Webb, Martin, G. (1996) *Winston Churchill: Using the tools of NLP to model his abilities* (now removed from the Web).

A useful NLP bibliography is available at
www.nlpschedule.com/bookrevs/bibliog1.html

index